W9-BSR-931

THE RELIGION OF ISRAEL

IS VOLUME

65

OF THE

Twentieth Century Encyclopedia of Catholicism

UNDER SECTION

VI

THE WORD OF GOD

IT IS ALSO THE

16TH

VOLUME IN ORDER OF PUBLICATION

Edited by HENRI DANIEL-ROPS of the Académie Française

THE RELIGION OF ISRAEL

By ALBERT GÉLIN, P.SS.

Translated from the French by J. R. FOSTER

HAWTHORN BOOKS · PUBLISHERS · *New York*

 This book was manufactured in the United States of America and published simultaneously in Canada by McClelland & Stewart, Ltd., 25 Hollinger Road, Toronto 16. Original French edition, *L'Ame d'Israël dans le Livre*. © Librairie Arthème Fayard, 1957. The Library of Congress has catalogued The Twentieth Century Encyclopedia of Catholicism under card Number 58–14327. Library of Congress Catalogue Card No. for this volume: 59-8203.

NIHIL OBSTAT

Joannes M. T. Barton, S.T.D., L.S.S.

Censor Deputatus

IMPRIMATUR

Georgius L. Craven, Episcopus Sebastopolis,

Vicarius Generalis

Westmonasterii, die XXXI DECEMBRIS, 1958

CONTENTS

CHAPTER I

ISRAEL'S VARIED HISTORY

The first impression left on the historian by the two thousand years of Israel's growth and development is one of variety and continuity. It is the variety that we should like to emphasize first. During its long history the people of Israel went through various sociological stages which have all left their mark upon it; it is as if manifold human experiences all helped it to sustain better the rôle of witness which Providence, we may say, had bestowed upon it.

Israel's first experience was that of the nomadic life. Abraham and the patriarchs were nomads. But they bred sheep, not camels. They were not bedouins, who may die without seeing a town, for the camel is a robust animal which can survive for three days without a drink, and camel-rearing tribes are satisfied with wild country where water is scarce. The sheep is not so hardy as the camel; it cannot travel so far and it needs more water and better pasturage. That is why sheep-rearing tribes frequent sub-desert regions with a rainfall of one to two inches, the regions, in fact, where we meet the patriarchs in the Bible—Haran, Sichem, Bethel, Hebron and Beersheba. Pastoral scenes abound in stories like those introducing us to disputes about drinking-troughs (Gen. 29. 1–14) or to Jacob's secret method of multiplying his flocks (Gen. 30. 37–42). The little grey donkey, "one of the most permanent features of the Near East" (R. de Vaux), is also there (Gen. 24. 35, 22. 3); it was long to remain the mount of sheiks

(Gen. 49. 11; Judges 5; 10. 4), and attacks on the horse, the animal typifying the civilization that came later, are rooted in this fact (Zach. 9. 9). There we have just one detail testifying to the persistence in Israel's memory of the age of the patriarchs. Many others were preserved in everyday speech; a house was described as a "tent", "to pull up the tent pegs" signified "to start out" and "to load animals with their packs" meant "to get up early". The biblical theme of the shepherd and his flock springs from the same source (Ezech. 34; Ps. 74. 1; Jonas 10).

Abraham and the patriarchs did not settle in Palestine, which remained for them a land "in which they dwelt as strangers" (Gen. 17. 8). They wandered about as circumstances dictated, between the areas with settled populations, securing wells (Gen. 21. 25 ff.; 26. 18 ff.) and pastures (Gen. 32. 33). They had freely chosen the west by leaving Mesopotamia with other "men of the sands" (*Habirû*) of whose migration their own formed a part. Hence the name "Hebrews". This was about 1850 B.C.

A century later some nomadic groups followed the Hyksos to the delta of the Nile and, settling down with their flocks in the pasturages of the Wadi Tumilat, followed the fortunes of the invaders of Egypt. But the wheel of fortune turned and the Egyptian nationalistic reaction started to oppress these half-settled nomads, who once more came to feel a longing for the desert. Moses was the incarnation of this longing. He led out of the "house of slavery" Jacob's descendants, followed by a motley crew of tribes differing considerably in origin (Exod. 12. 38). This was the Exodus. It introduces us to a new and decisive experience in the nomadic life, in which the people of Israel was to take shape. The scene of this creative activity was the desert of Sinaï. Around a common sanctuary erected in the open air first at Sinaï, and later at Qadesh, Moses collected a federation of twelve tribes which, since Alt's work, has been compared to the ancient amphictyonies of Delos and Latium.[1] The federal tie was a religious one; it extended the natural tie already existing within any one tribe. Israel was a huge organism which had to test its strength for forty years. The centrifugal tendencies which became apparent enable us to understand the very delicate equilibrium of the system, which was to last, with some renewal of its constituent elements, until the tenth century B.C.

The tribe consists of all those who travel together: its name (*shebet*, *matte*) describes the staff of the leader who guides it. But the fabric of the tribe is already more artificial than that of the clan (*mishpaha*): a clan is a homogeneous community of people sharing the same blood, the same flesh and the same life. Abraham had only one clan. Moses' achievement consisted in binding disparate elements into a fraternal community, a people (the Hebrew term for which, *'am*, connotes intimacy) held together by family feeling. Its structure was oligarchical. Its leaders were judges and umpires, guardians of ancient custom, generals in war and discoverers of wells. They would normally possess the *beraka* (blessing), the vitality transmitted from generation to generation (Gen. 48. 15 ff.). To these responsible men were given names which tell us much; they were known as high ones (*nasi*), eminent persons (*nagid*), rams (*ayil*), nobles (*nadib*), libation pourers (*nasik*). God is referred to among nomads as El, he who walks in front, the Sheik.

The spiritual background to Israel's first upwards steps is one of aspiration amid a rarely perfect unity. Poetry expresses it best. At first it is mainly the work of the professional bards, the *moshelim* (Num. 21. 27), but sometimes, too, that of inspired persons like Miriam and Debora. Its movement and vigour spring from repetition, parallelism and rhythm. The

[1] An amphictyony was properly a religious association of Greeks worshipping at the same shrine. The author is here thinking of the Delian League and the Latin League which evolved into the Athenian (fifth century B.C.) and Roman empires respectively. [*Trans.*]

rhythm gives the poem affinities with music and dancing. It is open-air, communal lyricism, springing from collectively-shared feelings which it intensifies. It has something of the power of an incantation, stimulates to action and has been summed up as "an aspect of clan-life" (Causse).

It must be understood once for all that the Hebrew verse is based on the number of stresses, that is, tonic syllables. Among the ancient Greeks the fiddler, wearing a wooden boot, would stamp the ground at each strong beat. A similar stress-rhythm forms the basis of English verse. The old stories are dotted with fragments of this primitive, spontaneous literature. We meet work-songs, like this one for boring a well: "Here is the well that was dug by princes; the chieftains of the host laid it open with the staves they carried, with the giver of the law to lead them" (Num. 21. 17–18).

Then there are festive songs for marriages, like the one sung by Rebecca's brother: "Sister of ours, may thousands of thousands spring from thee, and may thy posterity storm the gates of their enemies" (Gen. 24. 60).

But the most common are war-chants, like this one of Lamech's, which seems to have been inherited from the Qenite[2] tribes: "The man that wounds me, the stripling who deals me a blow, I reward with death. For Cain, sevenfold vengeance was to be taken; for Lamech it shall be seventy times as much" (Gen. 4. 23–4).

When we read this wild chant we realize what a tremendous step forward towards the rule of law was signified by the law of retaliation, which introduced the principle of "an eye for an eye, a tooth for a tooth" into the vendetta. To take further examples, here is the federal war-cry, which occurs in a story in Exodus: "Lift up your hands to the Lord's throne! The Lord declares war against Amalec, for all ages to come" (Exod. 17. 16); and the choral song of victory, struck up by

[2] The Qenites (or Kenites) were a tribe living in Sinaï; they seem to have joined the Israelites. [*Trans.*]

Miriam and sung by the women after the crossing of the Red Sea: "A psalm for the Lord, so great he is and so glorious; horse and rider hurled into the sea!" (Exod. 15. 21).

At the amphictyonic meetings, each tribe boasted of its own achievements. That is the literary form at the basis of Gen. 49 and Deut. 33, but in these chapters Israel is in the process of settling in Canaan and it is the *moshelim* of the federation who distribute praise and blame. Debora did this on the occasion of a famous battle, which gave us the oldest long poem in the Bible. It is full of fierce joy (Judges 5) and, as far as I know, has never been used by the Christian Church in its liturgy.

In the desert the faculty of observation is sharpened. It has bequeathed to us miniature pictures full of humour. Prov. 30. 24–8 preserves traces of them: "Of four little things in nature, wise men cannot match the skill. How puny a race the ants, that hoard their food in harvest time; how defenceless the rock-rabbits, that hide their burrows in the clefts! No prince have the locusts, yet ever they march in rank; the lizard climbs high, and makes its home in the palace of kings."

These singers are also story-tellers. In the tents and at the annual festivals they would relate the glorious or sorrowful tales which were one day to be written down and organized into a coherent whole. The genius of Israel shines forth in these stories unequalled in the ancient east for psychological subtlety and evocative power. Just think of the story of Joseph with its undercurrent of emotion (Gen. 37–48), the rivalry of Jacob and Esau, with the satirical jab at the latter, who represents Edom (Gen. 27), or the description of the oppression of the Hebrews in Egypt, which is depicted as a sort of concentration camp (Exod. 1–2). It has been said that the civilizations of the ancient east produced chronicles and not history. But this apprenticeship in history has its roots in the old anonymous story-tellers. Causse discovered in the Hebrew genius "a real inferiority in powers of exposition and description". But really the essential point is that it displays such an interest in man and his behaviour.

Perhaps we have passed somewhat beyond the boundaries of this nomadic age which we simply wished to sketch. But then Israel was never to forget its origins, it was always to retain something of the democratic ideal of the desert, a sort of pride which was to tinge the preaching of its prophets and its messianic dreams. We shall see more clearly in the next chapter the spiritual exploitation of the "desert myth" by Elias and Osee. And as though to perpetuate the memory of olden days, even as late as the seventh century, the Rechabites[3] were still faithful nomads admired by Jeremias (Jer. 35).

The pastoral stage in Israel's history was succeeded by the agricultural stage. This is not the place to retrace the story of the tribes' settlement in Canaan. After Josue's initial victories it turned out to be a slow process. Obviously the native inhabitants did not disappear (Judges 2. 23); between them and the Israelites bonds were forged by marriage and treaty. The natives possessed the superficial advantage of an agricultural civilization, perfectly expressed and, as it were, animated by its fertility-religion. Farmers are not made overnight, and Israel had almost everything to learn: the calendar, the technique, country wisdom. *Graecia capta ferum victorem cepit* ("When Greece had been enslaved she made a slave of her rough conqueror"): in this case, too, the law neatly formulated by Horace (*Epistles*, 2. 1, line 156) proved valid, to the danger of Israel's religion, as we shall see later.

The genius of Israel is eclectic. That is one of its most constant characteristics. It might even be maintained that, from the religious point of view, that is one of the most comprehensible reasons why Israel was chosen by God. So the Hebrews became an agricultural people and their religion

[3] The Rechabites were a branch of the Qenites (or Kenites). See note on p. 10. [*Trans.*]

was adapted to their new situation. Deut. 26. 1–10 should be read as the ancient liturgy of the first fruits, in which, with deliberate emphasis, the Levite presents Yahweh as the dispenser of the blessings of the soil. Isaias 28. 23–9 even speaks of Yahweh as him who taught men the art of agriculture; in the same way in Egypt Thoth was regarded as the inventor of hieroglyphics, and in Phoenicia a god was regarded as the author and patron of navigation: "Plough the farmer must, ere he sow, but will he be ever ploughing? For hoe and harrow is there no rest? Nay, he will level it anon, plant fennel, sow cummin, with a border of wheat or barley, millet or vetch; such lore he has learned, such prudence his God has given him" (Isaias 28. 24–6).

To dwell in the land and live there in security (Ps. 37. 3), to accumulate wealth and prosperity in one's house (Ps. 112. 3), to throng in to take possession of Yahweh's gifts (Jer. 31. 12); those are the blessings and ideals reflected in the materialistic religion which the Old Testament long remained. But these extremely concrete "blessings" are not gained without toil. It is pleasant to hear in the oldest collections of Proverbs, which spring from a rural background, these exhortations to persevering work: "Wilt thou gather in harvest time, a son well schooled? Or sleep the summer round, to thy father's great shame" (10. 5). "Till field and fill belly; idle pursuits are but foolishness" (12. 11). "Too cold to plough, says Sloth; vainly, when harvest comes, he will go a-begging" (20. 4).

There is certainly no sympathy for the idler, as this little picture also shows: "Passing by field or vineyard where idleness reigned and improvidence, what sights I have seen! Nettles were everywhere, briars had covered the ground, the stone wall was ruinous. That sight I took to heart, found a warning in that ill example. Sleep on (thought I) a little longer, yawn a little longer, a little longer pillow head on hand; ay, but poverty will not wait, the day of distress will not wait; like an armed vagabond it will fall upon thee!" (Prov. 24. 30–4).

Our brothers the animals are not forgotten in these maxims reminiscent of Deuteronomy (Deut. 25. 4; 22. 6 ff.), as this observation shows: "A just man cares for the safety of the beasts he owns; the wicked are heartless through and through" (Prov. 12. 10).

Deuteronomy, a historical book dating in essence from the eighth century, expresses perfectly this rustic ideal. The theme of the inheritance (*nehala*) appears; we hear of a land "flowing with milk and honey" (Deut. 6. 3; 11. 9). This is a farmer's phrase, as the parallel conception found at Ras Shamra shows:

> "The heavens will rain fat,
> The streams flow with honey."

The wealth of the country is described in detail: "Cities great and fair, not of thy building; houses that abound in wealth, not of thy making, wells not of thy digging, vineyards and oliveyards not of thy planting" (Deut. 6. 10–11).

It is clear that the picture is complete: Israel is proud of its cities and especially of Jerusalem, the city of David, site from the tenth to the sixth centuries before Christ of a dynasty and a temple, visible signs of a permanence blessed by God and the pride of the rural population, which makes pilgrimages to see them: "Jerusalem, built as a city should be built that is one in fellowship. There the tribes meet, the Lord's own tribes. . . ." (Ps. 121. 3–4).

It is obviously a simplification to adopt, as we have done, the somewhat idealistic viewpoint of Deuteronomy. In fact centrifugal forces acting from within and the repeated attacks of the great empires led Israel to a catastrophe: the collapse of 586. That year saw the downfall of the Israelite state and its visible signs of power; Jerusalem was captured, the Temple burnt, the reigning dynasty dethroned and the governing classes led into exile at Babylon. A rural proletariat was left in a country deprived of any kind of organization, a proletariat which played no part in assuring the essential continuity between the Israel of the past and the Israel of the future.

The Exile may perhaps be regarded as the centre of gravity of Israel's whole history. Those fifty years or so (586–538), like the forty in the desert, mark the beginning of a new, twofold experience. Two very different but complementary figures are foreshadowed, the Zionist and the cosmopolitan Jew.

In the case of the second of these, Jeremias' advice to the exiles has certainly borne fruit. His words were: "Build yourselves houses to dwell in . . . grow numerous. . . . A new home I have given you; for the welfare of that realm be ever concerned . . ." (Jer. 29. 4 ff.). E. Fleg[4] has described the significance of this letter to the exiles; it has remained the charter of Jews absorbed by other countries. Previously, it is true, there had been settlements abroad—there were the silk merchants of Damascus (3 Kings 20. 34) and the military colonists at Elephantine in Egypt—but the phenomenon had remained a limited one and sympathy for foreigners played no part in it. The "wise men" were the only class in which relations with other countries were considered creditable; before the Exile religious circles regarded them with a somewhat jaundiced eye. Henceforth the Jew adopted the foreigner's mode of life; fifth-century documents of the firm of Murashu at Nippur—probably the inventors of the banker's cheque—show us Jews in a good social position, owning land and capital, and even employed as officials of the king of Persia. A decided inclination towards the liberal professions and business becomes evident. The cosmopolitan tendencies of the next few centuries and the "melting-pot" policy of the Hellenistic monarchs were to favour this tendency to

[4] *Pourquoi je suis juif*, Paris, 1928, p. 94.

"disperse" among the nations. Soon Jews were settled wherever the olive grew, that is, all round the Mediterranean, and Juvenal, in his satires, was able to maintain that business stopped at Rome on the Sabbath.

The leading characteristic of the Dispersion was great devotion to ancestral tradition; proof of this is to be seen in the book of Tobias, which is a homage to the family, the tried and tested centre of this devotion.

Apostates like those described in Wisdom 2 were to be rare. In fact, on to this taste for the world was to be grafted a proselytizing activity which will require further mention; the two missionary charters of the Old Testament proceed from these outward-looking circles.

The Zionist tendency—the term is not an anachronism—is expressed during the Exile in the patriotic Psalm 136: "We sat down by the streams of Babylon and wept there, remembering Sion."

An *élite* started to return from Exile from 538 onwards and little by little inaugurated at Jerusalem something quite fresh, a Church. Jerusalem and the surrounding countryside no longer represented a political force but sheltered a community cultivating the spiritual life. Jerusalem now became the Holy City (Isaias 52. 1). The Temple and the Law were the centres of interest, as we can see from Malachias (*c.* 450 B.C.) or Ecclesiasticus (*c.* 200 B.C.). That is only an outline of events. The flame of nationalism certainly blazed up again from time to time, either in imagination (Ecclus. 36. 1–19) or in reality (the Machabees). A semi-racial exclusiveness (Esdras 10) accompanied this movement, as though to protect it. There is no need, for the moment, to emphasize these false steps which did not hold up the advance as a whole.

The holy centre of Jerusalem is in contact with the network of the Dispersion, whose cohesion it guarantees. Every year the *hadjis* come to this Mecca with their prayers and presents: "Praise the Lord, the Lord is gracious; his mercy endures for ever; be this the cry of men the Lord has rescued, rescued them from the enemy's hand, and gathered them in from sunrising and sunset, from the north country and the south" (Psalm 106. 1–3).

There began to take shape the vision of a world grouped round Jerusalem, the religious metropolis of the universe: "All must claim Sion as their birthplace. None was ever born, the proverb shall run, that did not take his birth from her" (Psalm 86. 5).

CHAPTER II

THE PEOPLE OF THE COVENANT

We have already passed beyond the borders of purely sociological or psychological investigation, for it is almost impossible to deal with the *historical problem* of Israel without touching on the *mystery* of Israel. Whether wandering in the desert, tilling the soil or dispersed among the cities of the world, this people carries a secret on which it lives, a vocation which it receives and discovers, a vocation which gives spiritual unity to its history. We must look beyond empirical reality and bow to this inner force by presenting Israel as the people of the Covenant.

This people with no real talent for philosophical thought, no scientific achievements of any sort to its credit and no important contribution to make to humanity's artistic heritage, was yet the one chosen by God to be his partner and witness: "God has chosen what the world holds foolish" (1 Cor. 1. 26).

The next question must be, who is this God whose massive imprint can be seen on every page of the Bible? He is not the God of the philosophers, as Pascal points out, nor Aristotle's Prime Mover, who has no contact with men, nor Voltaire's divine locksmith, nor again the queer old God criticized by Marx, a real substitute product which our modern Prometheuses can stand up to without presumption. The God of the Bible is above all the living God, he who is not mocked—*Deus non irridetur* (Gal. 6. 7)—is not answerable for his actions (Rom. 11. 33–4) and is to be feared. The word fear in this context does not imply fright; it expresses a feeling of respect that cannot be likened to any other emotion. This attitude of fear—and trembling—is common to those great worshippers, Abraham, Moses and Job. The "holiness" of God is first of all a metaphysical quality differentiating him from all else; Isaias discovers it when he hears the seraphim proclaim it, and he becomes aware at the same time of his own position as a creature and a sinner (Isaias 6. 5–7). But this God is also the God who runs after humanity (Luke 15. 20), the God who enters history, the Holy One of Israel (Os. 11. 9), who begins a dialogue with his creatures, who knows them far better than they know him (Gal. 4. 9), the divine Father—in Tertullian's words, *Nemo tam Pater*—whose shattering interventions are described in the Bible, a God who loves (*agape*[1]) and wishes to be loved in return.

The Bible is simultaneously the revelation and the discovery of this God, who can stand up to confrontation with the Baals of Canaan as well as to the test of the Exile. He is first of all the God of Abraham, the "God of our Fathers", a tutelary God whose relations with the members of the clan take precedence over any he may have with a particular place or natural phenomenon. He protects the lives and travels of the patriarchs; he is the God of the Election, that spiritual pact marking the dawn of the history of salvation (Gen. 12. 1–3). But Abraham is only a prelude, with which Moses expressly claims continuity in the desert of Exodus (Exod. 36). The God of our Fathers was henceforth to be called Yahweh.

His greatness is crystallized in his name. Yahweh means "He who is truly and really there", the God who intervenes

[1] Agape (ἀγάπη) is the word used in the N.T. to denote "*charity*" and "*the love of God for man*". [*Trans.*]

and acts, the God who is always close at hand. We are to see that clearly in the epic of the desert, the fighting of wars and the expression of categorical or casuistical right. "Who shall doubt the Lord's power?" thunders his prophet in days to come (Ezech. 6. 13; 7. 27; 11. 10).

The name corresponds to a kind of intensification of personality. It is a sort of power which dwells on the people (Num. 24. 27), the Temple (Jer. 7) or the prophet (Jer. 15). It may be that this name existed already in the traditions of certain Israelite tribes (Levi or Juda, for example), or even over a far larger Semitic area; L. Köhler and H. H. Rowley maintained that it was borrowed from the Qenites. None the less, the revelation of the burning bush remains something essentially new: the consciousness of a mastery and power that would assert itself in history and carry its plans to a successful conclusion, respect for the God of hosts who moves heaven and earth to lead the Israelite battalions to victory, fear at the demands of this God, the fount of morality, who intervenes in history with his blessing or his wrath. He has no sex and no myth. He cannot be represented; primitive Yahwism is characterized by a reaction against any kind of image. He cannot be seen; chapter 33 of Exodus is the *locus classicus* for the *Deus absconditus*. It is known that his mysterious manifestations, noted by the theologically-minded as "an angel of Yahweh", "the face of Yahweh", "the glory of Yahweh", are only partial aspects of his full being. He cannot be grasped, and the mobility of the ark, his portable sanctuary, is a concrete symbol of his omnipresence. What was important was to emphasize his spiritual nature. If human feelings were attributed to him, that was only to steer clear of rationalistic deism and to preserve the idea of the living God.

Yahweh alone is sufficient. There is no need for his people to invoke a number of gods in order to enjoy varied and extraordinary assistance; it might be said of him, as it is of Wisdom (Wisdom 7. 22), that he is the universal specialist. So he permits no division of worship: "Never pay worship to any alien god; the very name of the Lord (*qanna*) bespeaks jealous love, he will endure no rival" (Exod. 34. 14). This exclusiveness demands in practice an attitude of "monoyahwism".

The objective criterion by which the great monotheistic movements are distinguished is the express denial of any other god, as in Isaias 45. 5, or in the Islamic *shahada* ("There is no god but Allah"). But obviously one can feel and act as a monotheist without a clear and explicit definition of this sort, whose formulation postulates a certain level of culture and especially the advent of the "logical age", placed by W. F. Albright somewhere about the sixth century B.C. Moses is unquestionably a monotheist.

In the eyes of the Old Testament Yahweh becomes at the same time the Saviour and first member of a community founded by him. That is the economy of the Covenant.

The word Covenant (*berit*, Akkadian *birtu*) denotes the very strong bond uniting partners; the sharing of a meal, the exchange of blood or clothes inaugurate and symbolically create this new human relationship expressing friendship, mutual support and a sort of kinship. God makes use of an established custom and gives it a new validity. He cannot be a partner on equal terms; it is he who authorizes the Covenant, so that it always appears as an initiative of his grace. The other partner then receives the blessed name of Israel, which means "How strong is God"! Such a name is a sort of prayer, and an admission of weakness; it is the baptismal name of a people whose confidence in life and history was to proceed, as Pedersen has pointed out, less from what it had done than from what it had received. When it received this name Israel came into existence as a people. Later, the author of Deuteronomy was to speak of a divine redemption (*padah*) which brought it into being. The redemption from Egypt is a break with a sinful world and leads to the creation of a people apart.

Henceforth Yahweh stakes everything on its cohesion; Israel is the unit of salvation and the individuals of which it is composed have to behave as befits members of a great group chosen by God as his witness, his first fruits (*reshit*) (Jer. 2. 2), his first-born (*bekor*) (Exod. 4. 22). God's people is defined in an interesting passage in Deuteronomy (7. 6–11), in which the characteristic transition from "you" to "thou" should be noted:

> Yours is a people set apart for its own God, chosen by its own God, out of all the nations on earth, as his own people. If the Lord has held you closely to him and shewed you special favour, it was not that you overshadowed other peoples in greatness; of all nations you are the smallest. No, it was because the Lord loved you, because he was true to the oath which he had sworn to your fathers, that he delivered you by force, reclaimed you from the slave's life you were living in the power of Pharao king of Egypt. And thou wilt find it ever the same; the Lord thy God is God almighty, is God ever faithful; if men will love him and keep his commandments, he is true to his word, and shews mercy to them while a thousand generations pass; if they make him their enemy, his speedy retribution overwhelms them, brings them, without more ado, the reward they have deserved.

For the Covenant lays on Israel a special responsibility. It must do honour to the name it bears and not draw on itself the reproach so often uttered by Ezechiel: "You profane my name before the nations." The fact of the Covenant lies at the root of the determined self-criticism and persevering efforts to make the conception "God's people" a living reality. One of these efforts is enshrined in the book of Deuteronomy. Confronted with the disintegration of Israel in the eighth century, legislators take up old Mosaic texts and present them with eloquent appeals to the heart. The idea is to re-create Israel, that is, "a people of brothers", an exclusive people perhaps, but one full of human warmth and inspired by charity. Social legislation aims at establishing regular contributions in support of the disinherited (14. 28–9), enforcing respect for aliens, Levites, orphans and widows (24. 17–18; 15. 7–8; 23. 24–5: right to eat neighbour's grapes; 24. 19–22: gleaning rights), and easing the relationship between debtor and creditor (24. 6, 10–13) or employer and servant (24. 14–15). Equalizing laws, septennial remission of debts (15. 1–11) and liberation of slaves (15. 12–15) aim in theory at the maintenance of a middle class. The king himself is called upon to observe the bounds of moderation (17. 14–20). This somewhat ideal society might be described as keeping the Covenant.

Thus Yahweh calls on his people to collaborate with him, for although the Covenant is a grace it also implies effort. The task consists of establishing the kingdom of God on earth by inaugurating it at home before spreading it abroad. Israel the witness will then become Israel the mediator.

It is hardly necessary to emphasize that the Covenant is a divine educational operation which is ultimately universal in scope. "First-fruits" (Jer. 2. 3) can only be understood by reference to the harvest, and "first-born" (Exod. 4. 22) implies brothers. The whole Bible is universalist in attitude; God cares for the whole of humanity which he holds by the root in Adam. The choice of Abraham does not mean that other races are neglected; they will be blessed one day in him (Gen. 12. 3), and God reveals himself to them through the stars (Rom. 1. 19–20) and the voice of conscience (Rom. 2. 15–16). But Israel has been chosen as a sort of filter in which the religious strivings of humanity as a whole are to be canalized and purified. Hence its genius for assimilation, its eclecticism. It should be no cause for surprise if we meet in the Bible so many faint traces of humanity itself on the move towards God. Its myths may become the literary clothing of revelation (Ps. 74. 12–14), the vetoes and taboos of its first attempts at morality are transformed into commandments (Ezech. 18. 6), methods of divination are refined into "signs", magic itself still lingers on here and there in the Bible (e.g. Num. 5. 11–31) before being completely eliminated from it, the sacrificial system is partly borrowed and the very prayers of Babylon and Egypt find echoes in the liturgy of the chosen people. Israel's roots go deep into the humanity of which it was to form the religious apex. The comparative method of study demanded by the circumstances serves only to emphasize Israel's superiority in this field.

The prophets explained the Covenant by comparing it to a marriage. Besides giving this religious experience an emotional overtone, they thus taught that it was a task to be accomplished in common, for Yahweh and Israel are wedded to each other, and the metaphors of betrothal, seduction, adultery, divorce and reconciliation describe the fluctuation and vicissitudes of the union. Osee, in the eighth century, was the first to exploit this image to the full. The tale of his own married life was the divinely-inspired symbol of a more admirable story. He fell in love with a sacred prostitute and married her. There is no evidence to suggest that the marriage did not turn out well, but it is a justifiable assumption that Gomer never attained the level of Osee. The application was easy. Yahweh speaks of Israel and to Israel in moving words: "It is but love's stratagem, thus to lead her out into the wilderness; once there, it shall be all words of comfort" (Osee 2. 14). "Everlastingly I will betroth thee to myself, favour and redress and mercy of mine thy dowry; by the keeping of his troth thou shalt learn to know the Lord" (Osee 2. 19–20).

Similarly, Isaias puts on the lover's lips the song of love to his vineyard, the usual metaphor for the beloved. Osee's tone is also adopted by Jeremias in a long poem (Jer. 3. 1–5, 19–25; 4. 1–4). Still stronger emotion is generated by Ezechiel's picture of the little girl Israel abandoned in the fields and saved, cared for and finally married by Yahweh:

> Who but I found thee, as I passed on my way, blood-bespattered as thou wert, and trodden under foot; in that plight preserved thee, bade it live on, this defiled thing?
>
> Swift as the wild blossoms I bade thee grow; grow thou didst and thrive, and camest to woman's estate, the breasts formed, new hair shewing; and still thou wast all naked and blushing for thy nakedness. Who but I came upon thee, as I passed on my way? And already thou wert ripe for love; cloak of mine should be thrown about thee, to hide thy shame; my troth I plighted to thee, the Lord God says, and thou wert mine (Ezech. 16. 6–8).

With admirable delicacy the prophets emphasized that this betrothal was a grace from God, and from this point of view tried to convert Israel to humility and gratitude. It would be pleasant to follow many authors of repute in assigning some of the poems in the Song of Songs to the prophetical tradition, but, as has been shown, they must be regarded as belonging to the Wisdom literature. The loves they sing of are human, whatever allegorical meanings the Rabbis may have enriched them with later.

The Covenant is an always imperfect reality; its programme must be continually put into practice. The liturgy provided Israel with the means of keeping this basic spiritual fact in mind and of making it effective. It is unlikely that there was ever, as A. Weiser has maintained,[2] an annual feast of the Covenant, for all the religious feasts of Israel necessarily recalled this fundamental event. In the psalter, the proclamation of the terms of the Covenant constitutes a special literary form, to which Psalms 49, 80 and 94 belong. The responsibility for this proclamation had been Moses'; it was to pass to the judges, then to the priests of the central sanctuary, partly to the prophets and even, for archaistic reasons, to King Josias (4 Kings 23. 2). Jos. 24 is a very old account of a renewal of the Covenant at Sichem, when the tribes had gained

[2] *Die Psalmen*, Göttingen, 1950, 1952.

a foothold in Palestine. There were many others, including the one connected with Nehemias (2 Esdras 10) in the fifth century. The theme of *Today* echoes through the exhortations made on these occasions:

> Come in, then, fall we down in worship, bowing the knee before God who made us. Who but the Lord is our God? And what are we, but folk of his pasturing, sheep that follow his beckoning hand?
>
> Would you but listen to his voice today! Do not harden your hearts, as they were hardened once at Meriba, at Massa in the wilderness. Your fathers put me to the test, challenged me, as if they lacked proof of my power. (Ps. 94. 6–9.)

We have just named some of the men whose job it was to preserve the Covenant. The importance of these upholders of the tradition cannot be over-estimated; Israel was to remain strongly bound to its past so as to be able to face the future.

A. Neher[3] has shown the importance of the Levites. These professional priests formed the ancient backbone of the people; present everywhere, they bound each village to the tradition of the Exodus, which they preserved and expounded. They were the guardians of rites and customs and were largely responsible for the religious education of Israel. The old creed preserved in Deut. 26. 5–10 is probably their work, and the instructions for entrance, too, in which they defined the conditions to be fulfilled in order to appear before the face of Yahweh (Ps. 14). Moses praised them in advance: "Here are men who treated their own children as strangers, paying heed rather to thy warnings, keeping true to thy covenant. Here, they said to Jacob, are the decrees thou must obey, here, Israel, is the law that governs thee. When thou art angry, Lord, it is theirs to offer incense, and burn sacrifice upon thy altar" (Deut. 33. 9–10).

In continual contact with people, they do not speak in the thunderous and passionate tones of the prophets, but they

[3] *L'essence du prophétisme*, Paris, 1956.

agree with them on the fundamental point of loyalty to the past. The difference between priest and prophet is one of tone only and the opposition between the two which the nineteenth-century liberal school claimed to see has not found acceptance.

The prophets are revolutionaries whose watchword is the past. The priesthood was somewhat weighed down by the atmosphere of Canaan, even perhaps by the reception into its ranks of Canaanite priests, and certainly by its guardianship of the kings. It did not always escape contamination, as witness Osee. The prophets are people for whom tradition has become a living reality of which they are personally aware; and because of their experience of God they gave violent expression to this tradition. Their revolutionary ardour was loyalty to the past, but it was a creative loyalty.

The honour of officially keeping the Covenant finally fell to the king. Responsible for his people, God's lieutenant on earth, a priest by birth, he is, as it were, the official delegate to the Covenant, and this function defines his duties, of which the prophets are continually reminding him. This conception of the king, which originated with the prophecy of Nathan (2 Kings 7), explains both the people's pride in him and the disappointment he is liable to cause. The old royal psalms stop at the first of these two aspects of his position (Pss. 2, 71, 109); the prophets dwell at length on the second.

These people, the upholders of the Covenant, are also its living signs. There are others: the good land occupied by Israel, the capital, Jerusalem, with its temple whose guardian is the king, in accordance with Yahweh's words, "Here, on mount Sion, my sanctuary, I enthrone a king of my own choice" (Ps. 2. 6), the feasts regularly celebrated there, the paraphernalia of the State, its success and permanence, and finally the sabbath and circumcision, those institutions inherited from the distant past.

The day came when Israel had to say: "Our own emblems

are nowhere to be seen, there are no prophets left now. . . ." (Ps. 73. 9).

However, the date 586 B.C. was not to mark the end of the Covenant but the start of a better way of putting its terms into effect. Israel, Yahweh's partner, was to be kept alive in a new form. The confederation of the desert and the conquest had given way to a centralized and well-equipped monarchy, which had collapsed. Henceforward the watchword was to be quality. A community of people was going to fulfil the dream of Jeremias (31. 31–3):

> A time is coming, the Lord says, when I mean to ratify a new covenant with the people of Israel and with the people of Juda. It will not be like the covenant which I made with their fathers, on the day when I took them by the hand, to rescue them from Egypt; that they should break my covenant, and I, all the while, their master, the Lord says. No, this is the covenant I will grant the people of Israel, the Lord says, when that time comes. I will implant my law in their innermost thoughts, engrave it in their hearts; I will be their God, and they shall be my people.

In exile was to be formed an Israel based on quality and headed by the "poor of Yahweh" (Isaias 49. 13), the nucleus of the "remnant" and "the people set apart for the most High" (Dan. 7. 27) which forms, before the coming of Christ, the semi-ecclesiastical community of Jerusalem.

The dialogue structure of the religion has not changed; Yahweh simply converses with a people which responds better to its extraordinary vocation.

CHAPTER III

ISRAEL'S MORAL CODE

The moral aspect of biblical religion cannot fail to strike even the superficial reader of Scripture. We are confronted with a lofty morality right from the start, but gradually its edicts develop, its motives are refined and its demands go deeper.

Its originality lies less in its content than in its form. It is essentially a Covenant morality, and consequently assumes a dialogue structure. It consists of call and response uttered to the rhythm of a drama with whose principal players we are already familiar: "This, then, is the Lord's message to you, men of Israel, to the whole race I rescued from Egypt: Nation is none I have claimed for my own, save you; and guilt of yours is none that shall go unpunished" (Amos 3. 1–2).

In its earliest form this morality is bound up with the dominating figure of the Old Testament. It is not easy to classify Moses among the great leaders of men. "He stands apart, a leader of primordial times, who spoke directly to Yahweh" (Pedersen). The ancient accounts show him as God's interlocutor, speaking to him "face to face" (Num. 12. 8), and as a very human sheik carrying Israel on his breast like a nurse (Num. 11. 12).

His purpose was to bind together and organize a growing society which remained friable in the fluid conditions of the desert. The Decalogue is "the formulation of Moses' ancient rule for his community" (Sellin). It has only been preserved in a highly developed and somewhat overloaded form and in two slightly different versions (Exod. 20. 1–17 and Deut. 5. 6–18), but it is not difficult to strip it of later explanatory accretions and to restore the primitive and lapidary form of the "ten commandments". The two tables on which they were inscribed conveniently contained the sacred and profane law of a society which they reminded of the bond which held it together, the primordial principles of its life and the rhythm of its repose:

I. I am Yahweh thy God, who rescued thee from the land of Egypt, from slavery: thou shalt not have any other gods besides me.
II. Thou shalt not make any idols.
III. Thou shalt not take the name of Yahweh thy God in vain.
IV. Keep the sabbath day holy.
V. Honour thy father and mother.
VI. Thou shalt not kill.
VII. Thou shalt not commit adultery.
VIII. Thou shalt not steal.
IX. Thou shalt not bear false witness against thy neighbour.
X. Thou shalt not covet thy neighbour's goods.

We can deduce from these commandments the character and orientation of the morality they inaugurate. It is a morality based on gratitude, gratitude to Yahweh whose blessings and demands become apparent at the birth of Israel as a people. His very demands appear as a favour, for the law is a grace and, in a rabbi's words, "its commandments are the reason for Israel's existence".

It is also a morality of categorical imperatives. Biblical morality is not a humanistic construction, a technique of personal achievement and social equilibrium. It is part of the divine word which must be accepted or rejected. It presupposes a summons from God to man. The human response is obedience or refusal; the latter attitude implies actual opposition to God, a check to his will. There is a specifically biblical term to express it, the word *pesha'*, which more or less implies defiance: "Listen, you heavens, and let earth attend to this, a divine remonstrance; my own sons, that I reared and brought to manhood, hold me in defiance!" (Isaias 1. 2).

In biblical terminology, sin is something positive and aggressive. It is contrasted with the eager willingness of faith and obedience. But both willingness and refusal are judged by reference to precise injunctions, formulated in an apodeictic style, which have no parallel outside Israel. God harries his people.

Or rather he invites and guides it. The word *Torah* preserves the memory of these instructions and invitations (it comes from the *warah* root, which means to show the way, point out). The morality expressed in the Decalogue is only the beginning of this Torah, whose splendid edifice was to rise during the next thousand years on the essential foundation laid by the first legislator, thanks to a development starting from within. Right from Moses' time biblical morality is a morality calculated to preserve the unity of a people and to initiate it into the life of holiness. But it is not difficult to see that the pedagogic principle already at work was to produce other results. The two versions of the Decalogue mentioned above already bear witness to this expository work to which we shall return later.

This morality of preservation was at the same time a morality of separation. We emphasized above the close relations of Israel with neighbouring civilizations, but we must not on that account forget the principle of *Abgrenzung* stressed so much by Hempel.[1] In opposition to the neighbouring countries, Israel has its own rhythm of work and rest, its own original liturgy, a sexual morality very different from the

[1] *Das Ethos des Alten Testaments*, Berlin, 1938.

horrors it was to witness and a phobia of the magic prevalent all round it. The holy people is also the people set apart (Lev. 19. 1). This ἀμιξία (*amixia*, unwillingness to mix), scoffed at later by pagan writers, is already foreshadowed in the Decalogue: "Here is a people destined to dwell apart, not counted among the muster-roll of the nations" (Num. 23. 9).

It is difficult to speak of biblical morality without bringing in the tradition that preserved and developed it. The tradition entrusted to Moses' heirs, to men endowed like him with special graces (Josue, the judges) and to the Levites, was essentially a sacred one.

In exceptional circumstances it was felt desirable to renew the Covenant. The account in Jos. 24 preserves the memory of a celebration of this kind at Sichem in the twelfth century, and in 4 Kings 11. 17 that of a renewal in the ninth century at the temple in Jerusalem, organized by the priest Joiada. In 4 Kings 23. 3, King Josias, in the seventh century, rather exceptionally reserves this task for himself. Regular renewals also took place every year and the psalter preserves three psalms used on these occasions (Ps. 49, 80 and 94). In the ritual the primordial fact of the Covenant is re-enacted; Israel gathers at Yahweh's invitation to hear his voice: "Muster in my presence my faithful servants, who honour my covenant still with sacrifice" (Ps. 49. 5).

A liturgy of this sort is not merely commemorative; the priests continually remind their audience of the present (Ps. 94. 8) and republish in Yahweh's name the moral injunctions repeated since Sinaï:

> Listen, my people, to these words of mine, listen, Israel, to the protestation I make thee. . . .
>
> How is it that thou canst repeat my commandments by rote, and boast of my covenant with thee, and thou, all the while, hast no love for the amendment of thy ways, casting every warning of mine to the winds? Swift thou art to welcome the

thief who crosses thy path, to throw in thy lot with the adulterers. Malice wells up from thy lips, and thy tongue is a ready engine of deceit; thou wilt sit there in conclave, speaking evil of thy brother, traducing thy own mother's son. Such were thy ways, and should I make no sign? Should I let thee think I am such as thou? (Ps. 49. 7, 16–21).

The literary form of the proclamation of the Covenant's terms is not very different from another kind of literature in which the priest also appears. It is known as the liturgy of entry, and lists the conditions for entry to the sanctuary (Ps. 14). The remarkable thing is that the leading characteristic of all the passages mentioned is their faithfulness to the ethical tone of the Decalogue.

The prophets, too, bore witness to the same sacred tradition, not only by imitating the literary form of the proclamation of the Covenant's terms (as we see from Isaias 1. 10–17, 33. 14–16 and Mich. 6. 1–8), but also by taking an active part in the festivals, their speeches at which belong to the tradition of worship. Attention has recently been drawn to this fact with reference to Jeremias. The prophet reminds the people of Juda, on the occasion of a festival, of the contents of the Decalogue: "Theft, murder, adultery, the false oath, libations to Baal, the courting of alien gods that are no gods of yours, nothing comes amiss, if only you can come and stand in my presence . . ." (Jer. 7. 9–10).

But Jeremias goes further. In his view, ritual is only of secondary importance; and that is the implication of the sacred tradition itself, as expressed in the Decalogue. No doubt there is no religion without sacrifice—neither Israel nor Moses thought that (Exod. 24. 5)—but the Covenant was primarily concerned with ethics rather than ritual. We have only to listen to Yahweh himself:

No more be at pains to distinguish between burnt-sacrifice and offering; use for your own eating the flesh of all alike! Burnt sacrifices, offerings, not of these was my theme when I gave commandments to your fathers at the time of their deliverance from Egypt; my word of command to them was, Obey my bidding, if I am to be your God, you my people; follow the path I have marked out for you, as you hope to prosper. (Jer. 7.21–3.)

A century earlier, another prophet, Osee, had fiercely rebuked the priests as those responsible for the absence of "knowledge of God" in the land. This "knowledge of God" is synonymous with observation of the Decalogue; if people "curse and lie, murder and steal and live adulterously" (Osee 4. 2), that is because the priesthood is failing in its function: "Ruin for thee, sir priest, this day . . ." (Osee 4. 5). "Through thy fault, this people of mine perishes for want of knowledge. Knowledge wouldst thou spurn, and shall I not spurn thy priesthood" (Osee 4. 6).

Thus, whether they follow it, preach it or castigate the Levites who are its born defenders (Deut. 33. 10), the prophets are witnesses to a moral tradition going back to the origins of Israel.

Nor did they rest content with championing it at a time when any compromise with the morality of Canaan had to be clearly rejected. They also deepened it and at the same time simplified it by reducing it to basic attitudes implicit in the logic of the Covenant.

We must not forget that the Covenant is a meeting and exchange, an invitation and a communion. It aims at mutual acquaintance or "knowledge" and is expressed in terms of a relationship (*Verhältnisbegriffe*) binding God and man. The attitude of God towards Israel is summed up in the words justice (*sedeq*), kindness (*hesed*) and faithfulness (*emet*). But he expects this attitude to be reciprocated. For man, knowing God means adopting God's ways and modelling his behaviour on the divine pattern, for God has entered the sphere of humanity and disclosed to men the essentials of his attitude towards them. Henceforth, morality may be expressed, to use A. Neher's expression, in the imitative as well as in the imperative mood. Not that this ultimate moral ideal is pitched too high. Jer. 9. 24 is sufficient to reassure us on that score: "Boast is none worth having, save that insight which gives knowledge of me; in all my dealings with mankind so merciful a Lord, the Lord says, so just, so faithful, and a lover of such dealings where they are found." And in his diatribe against Joachim the same prophet recalls this king's predecessor in a contrasting picture: "Well for him that he gave the friendless and the poor redress, as men will when they bethink themselves of me" (Jer. 22. 16).

The divine preference for the poor is expressly held up for Israel's imitation, for, even in the Old Testament, if "the hidden meaning of morality is the relationship to God, the criterion by which it will be judged is the relationship to others" (Ricoeur), and many a page in the old Covenant foreshadows the words of St John: "If a man boasts of loving God, while he hates his own brother, he is a liar. He has seen his brother, and has no love for him; what love can he have for the God he has never seen?" (1 John 4. 20).

So the true Israelite can say to Yahweh: "Ever I keep thy mercies (*hesed*) in mind, ever thy faithfulness (*emet*) bears me company" (Ps. 25. 3) and make his own the watchwords of Michaeas: "Nay, son of Adam, what need to ask? Best of all it is, and this above all the Lord demands of thee, right thou shouldst do, and ruth love, and carry thyself humbly in the presence of thy God" (Mich. 6. 8).

Behind these apparently abstract terms we should try to feel the presence of the living God and to hear already the words of Matt. 5. 48: "But you are to be perfect, as your heavenly Father is perfect."

By promulgating such a lofty and concrete ideal of sanctity, God forestalled what has been called "the just man's sin", the belief that one has fulfilled every demand, for how can such a model be equalled? He also prepared the way for the incarnation of his Son, who in the New Covenant was to serve as a model revealing the Faith. "What the Father does is what the Son does in his turn" (John 5. 19). And finally he presented the imitation of God in terms which respected the primacy of the person and the primacy of action; the old Greek intellectual dream of ὁμοίωσις τῷ θεῷ (*homoiosis to theo*, assimilation to God) was thus to be simultaneously fulfilled and freed of its dangers.

One further comment is necessary. Ezechiel, with his catalogue of sins, and later the Pharisees, with their minute classification of errors, may create the impression of a too legalistic moral code. But a moral code can scarcely exist without the definition of offences against it; the divine will is encountered through the medium of concrete acts. Alongside his meticulous legalism, Ezechiel betrays evidence of a prophetical morality of heart and will inherited from his master Jeremias. Perhaps these two tendencies in the priest-prophet are an indication of the tension in every human heart. The imperative mood and the imitative mood exist simultaneously rather than consecutively.

But the logic of the Covenant demands even more than this. The initiative comes from God. It is he who bestows this grace on Israel and summons her into his own presence, holy and without stain (Ephes. 5. 7). To be sure, God must be imitated, but is such an imitation possible without the help of the original to be copied? Osee 2. 19–20 is probably the most pregnant passage that has been written on this subject. It looks forward to the messianic age, when "knowledge" of God will be perfect—its constituents are named—but only possible through the grace of God, symbolized in the image of a fresh marriage: "Everlastingly I will betroth thee to myself, favour and redress (*sedeq*) and mercy of mine (*hesed*) thy dowry; by the keeping of his troth (*emunah*) thou shalt learn to know the Lord."

Biblical morality is here expressed in terms of participation, in the participial mood, as it were. This conception removes any temptation which may assail biblical man to feel pride in the morality of his own actions. He is master of them, the Lord himself has treated him as a free agent and he has frequently heard the words, "It is not above thy reach, it is not beyond thy compass, this duty which I am now enjoining upon thee" (Deut. 30. 11). Ezechiel was by no means the first to rely on his capacity for conversion and constancy: "(Acquire) a new heart, a new spirit!" (Ezech. 18. 31). It is hardly surprising if he finally begins to take pride in himself, to seek there the fount of origin of his moral code and, in short, to be a pharisee, convinced that his "justice" is a purely human achievement. "The Lord has requited me" (Ps. 17. 25; cf. Phil. 3. 9) is one of the slogans of that Jewish wilfulness which, in its extreme form, was to claim to cultivate its own sanctity and to prepare ears of corn which the divine harvester had only to reap.

On this point, Israel had to learn that the reality was somewhat harsher and came to realize, from actual experience of sin, the need to apply for divine help. Here, too, the prophets rendered assistance, especially Jeremias. He diagnosed in his generation an incurable state of sin, a sinful condition rooted in the uncircumcised heart (Jer. 2. 25; 17. 1). So, in the future prepared by God, the heart was to be made receptive to an initiative from on high which would grant a fresh moral start through pardon, and the possibility of a more elevated spiritual life by means of mysterious inspirations and impulses; Israel was thus to have a new "heart" (Jer. 24. 7; 31–34). Following Jeremias, Ezechiel declared even more clearly that this "heart" would be a gift of God: "I will make my spirit penetrate you, so that you will follow in the path of my law, remember and carry out my decrees" (Ezech. 36. 27). The perfect moral life can only be achieved in a spiritual climate of grace. Probably no prayer throws more light on biblical man than the *Miserere*, that psalm in which Luther caught a Pauline note, because it is all appeal and "invocation": "My God, bring a clean heart to birth within me; breathe new life, true life into my being . . . do not take thy holy spirit away from me . . . and strengthen me in generous resolve" (Ps. 50. 12, 13, 14).

The announcements of Jeremias and Ezechiel have been brought up to date by this psalmist, their disciple. Gradually we meet more and more formulas presenting biblical man in communion with God, the recipient of a grace which enriches him and follows him in all his activities. The "Confessions" of Jeremias and the psalms of the *anawim*[2] are the vivid record of a life finding its source and its support in God. The wonders of grace, to be fully revealed in Jesus Christ, are already foreshadowed.

Biblical morality is a Covenant morality. That is its basis and originality, as priests and prophets have continually emphasized. But they were not the only people in Israel to concern themselves with morality. There was also the guild of "wise men". Their existence is not a specifically Hebrew phenomenon. Almost everywhere in the Near East there were schools for the transmission of wisdom, that is, the art of living one's life in accordance with certain norms of prudence, morality and religion. These schools were sometimes situated, as at Mari,[3] in temples. So even in the ancient civilizations scribes were moulded in a sort of university atmosphere. Today we have a fairly clear picture of the various departments in which the Sumerian sages excelled: "Strength and wisdom do not go together. . . . Pleasure in drinking means

[2] For the *anawim* or "poor of Yahweh", who played an important part in the religious life of post-exilic Israel, see Chapter IV. [*Trans.*]

[3] The modern Tell-Harīrī on the middle Euphrates. Mari was the capital of a powerful Amorite state conquered by Hammurabi *c.* 1695 B.C. A rich hoard of tablets found there has thrown much light on the patriarchal age. [*Trans.*]

fatigue on the road. . . . As long as I live I am tied like an ox. . . ."

These scribes formed a respected class of educated men. The state made use of them as civil servants, ministers and diplomats. They acted as links between different civilizations, for they enjoyed travelling and spoke foreign languages. The kingdom of Israel, modelled on other similar kingdoms, called on their services, and as early as David's time we find at the court the scribe Susa or Shavsha (1 Par. 18. 16), with his Babylonian name. The development of a bureaucracy in the Egyptian style from Solomon's reign onwards stimulated the development of a whole literature, to which the oldest collections of Proverbs belong (10–22, 16, 25–9), treating of life and morals.

The unfortunate part was that the circles of wise men provoked the criticism of the prophets, those vigilant censors of theocracy. The two sides were not using the same wavelength. Wisdom seemed a quality of dubious worth, for it remained the supreme political virtue; it is by no means certain that the title of "wise" accorded to David and Solomon was the expression of an unmixed admiration. The clubs of wise men find favour neither with Isaias (5. 21; 10. 13; 19. 11; 29. 14) nor with Jeremias (9. 11). Yet both were certainly capable of using the vocabulary of wisdom to convey their message about the nature of God (Isaias 28. 23–9) or the human heart (Jer. 17. 9–10). So the two points of view merged easily. There is nothing surprising in that, for Moses had been trained as an Egyptian scribe and was familiar with the morality to be found in the Book of the Dead (Chap. 125) and with the cult of Ma'ât (Truth and Virtue) of which it is the expression. The Decalogue is in contact with this universal code of ethics. Similarly, the preaching of an international morality and law in Amos 1–2 is probably due to the influence of the wise men. It is doubtless a mistake to erect rigid barriers between people whose work as moralists followed different paths but reached much the same conclusions. The removal of landmarks is equally deplored by Levite (Deut. 19. 14; 27. 17), prophet (Osee 5. 10) and sage (Prov. 22. 28; 23. 10, 11).

As a matter of fact, the wisdom literature does not put morality directly in line with the Covenant; it emphasizes the individual rather than the people as a whole, universalism rather than election, and merit rather than grace. It is a form of humanism which, although not devoid of the religious note, was only completely assimilated and approved after the Exile. It looks as though it was the influence of Jeremias that was decisive in establishing the new orientation; he made religious problems personal ones. It so happened that the conduct of one's own life, suffering and individual assent were all matters of particular interest to the wisdom literature, so that the attitude of Jeremias was extremely favourable to it. After the return from exile the old collections of proverbs were provided with a splendid prophetic and priestly introduction, Proverbs 1–9. From then onwards "fear of Yahweh", that is, religion, became more explicitly the "foundation of true wisdom" (Prov. 1–7) and the importance of the wise men continued to grow. Pious men, they may have become, as Mowinckel thinks, the editors of the Psalter. They were certainly the authors of several votive psalms, set up their schools near the Temple (Ecclus. 51. 13 ff.) and turned again to the national themes (Ecclus. 24: the Law; 36: the messianic expectation).

But their main literary activity was traditionally didactic poetry (the *mashal*). The term, which is not so clear as what it denotes, seems to express the simultaneously suggestive and concrete character of Israel's genius in its bent for teaching rather than the sense of comparison which some scholars would like to see in the root. Israel's didactic side is to be found in Proverbs (tenth to fifth century), Job (fifth to fourth century), Ecclesiasticus (second century), Baruch 3. 9 to 4. 4

(second century) and a number of psalms known as the sapiental psalms (1, 111, 127).

How far Wisdom was assimilated by Yahwism is best shown by the splendid poem known as the Infanta's Song:

> The Lord made me his when first he went about his work, at the birth of time, before his creation began. Long, long ago, before earth was fashioned, I held my course. Already I lay in the womb, when the depths were not yet in being, when no springs of water had yet broken; when I was born, the mountains had not yet sunk on their firm foundations, and there were no hills; not yet had he made the earth, or the rivers, or the solid framework of the world. I was there when he built the heavens, when he fenced in the waters with a vault invisible, when he fixed the sky overhead, and levelled the fountain-springs of the deep. I was there when he enclosed the sea within its confines, forbidding the waters to transgress their assigned limits, when he poised the foundations of the world. I was at his side, a master-workman, my delight increasing with each day, as I made play before him all the while; made play in this world of dust, with the sons of Adam for my playfellows. (Prov. 8. 22–31.)

A surprise awaits anyone who examines the text in which the rules for Israel's conduct are laid down. In the midst of moral precepts appear commands which have nothing to do with ethics. Numerous sexual taboos (Lev. 15. 16–24; 12. 2), rules governing contact with corpses and lepers, prohibitions about food and eating blood—various vetoes of the sort that we encounter in many primitive civilizations. Sociologists often introduce modern preoccupations, especially hygiene, into their explanations of these pointless regulations. In general, it is fair to say that they form a brake on a number of instinctive impulses and bear witness to the discipline which was perhaps the earliest aspect of morality. By welcoming them and changing them into commandments, the Bible once more performs its function of forming a link with the oldest human societies. In spite of the tendency, especially in Deuteronomy, to rationalize taboos, the fact remains that their abitrary nature enables Israel to appreciate more clearly the austerity of God's leadership. As Franz Rosenzweig puts it, "Do not say: I do not like pork! Say: I should like it very much, but my Father in heaven has forbidden me to partake of it."

The God who speaks in Lev. 19. 2 (a body of legislation perhaps dating from the time of Isaias) is the God of Holiness: "Be holy, for I, Yahweh, your God, am holy." We are tempted to read into what follows a spiritual economy of separation: the Holy is what is apart, what is other. But the concept has been adapted to the Covenant and has taken on a moral colour: It expresses the perfection of God as well as his metaphysical position. That is why Lev. 19 can begin with a recapitulation of the Decalogue, the charter of the Covenant (3–4, 11–12), and continue with recommendations regarding justice (13, 15–16, 20–2, 35–6), directions enjoining charity (14, 17–18, 32–4), precepts concerning morality (29), regulations for rituals (5–8, 30) and also vetoes (27–8), taboos assimilated by Yahwism (9–10, 23–5) and warnings against magic (19, 26, 31). The whole material life of Israel is covered by the Covenant.

CHAPTER IV

A PRAYING PEOPLE

"Tell me how you pray and I will tell you what sort of a man you are." It is above all by watching biblical man at prayer that we shall understand his secret and the intensity of the dialogue with God to which the preceding chapters have already introduced us.

Our first task on adopting this new standpoint will be to dispose of two false conceptions which never found complete acceptance in the days of liberal criticism and have since provoked a healthy reaction.

The first of these conceptions claimed to be based on chronology. The theory was that there were two well-defined periods in the religious history of Israel, one characterized by collectivism, the other by individualism, and that the principle of an individual's relationship with God was only formulated after the exile, by Jeremias and Ezechiel. In earlier times, so we were told by Stade, "the religious unit was not the individual Israelite but the people of Israel as a whole". But with the exile, which destroyed traditional frameworks and supports, "the community seems to have dissolved into a mass of individual units, who go their own ways, each operating independently and responsible in a strictly individual way for its own salvation or damnation" (Charles). Now while it is certainly a fact that the break caused by the exile forced the individual to become more aware of his own religious function and worth, he remained none the less firmly rooted in the Israel that we have tried to define. The Day of Atonement,[1] which clearly postulates the representation of the people *per modum unius* (by means of one person), is only recorded after the exile (Lev. 16). Conversely, there is very ancient testimony to the importance of the individual, legislation was certainly obliged to envisage individual cases and the prophets had to aim their preaching at concrete cases. But proof is particularly abundant in the realm of piety. It was the custom to crystallize in children's names the certainty of being followed and protected by Someone who is at the source of life. Names like Abi-Nadab ("the Father is liberal" —1 Kings 7. 1), Eli-shama' ("God has heard"—Num. 1. 10), Yeho-yada' ("Yahweh knows"—2 Kings 8. 18), Pada-Iah "Yahweh redeems"—4 Kings 23. 36), Jo-achaz ("Yahweh takes"—4 Kings 23. 20) and Yedid-Iah ("beloved of Yahweh" —2 Kings 12. 25) are "as a general rule the expression of piety, even the simple and sincere piety of the individual. . . . The eminently individualistic point of view which sees in every man not only an object of the divine activity, but also an 'I' as opposed to a 'you', that is, a conscious personality, is expressed in these very old names. Personal names will always give the lie to any theory maintaining that in ancient times the relationship between the Godhead and the people was the only one that existed" (M. Noth). A. Wendel[2] has noted the diversity of the spontaneous prayers in which ancient Israel expressed its complete confidence in the "God of every day" (*Alltagsgott*). The most touching is perhaps that of the barren Anna coming, in the eleventh century, to the sanctuary of Silo to ask for a son:

> Sad at heart, she prayed to the Lord with many tears, and made a vow: Lord of hosts, if thou wilt take good heed of this

[1] A feast holding an important position in the Jewish calendar and known in later Judaism as *Yoma* ("the Day") or *Yoma Rabba* ("the Great Day"). [*Trans.*]

[2] *Das frei Laïengebet im vorexilischen Israël*, Leipzig, 1932.

> sorrow I bear, if thou wilt keep this handmaid of thine ever in remembrance, and grant her a son, then he shall be my gift to the Lord all his life long, a Nazirite unshorn. Such was the prayer she went on repeating, there in the Lord's presence; and Heli saw her lips moving as she did so; her lips pronounced the secret petition, but with no sound. Heli though her besotted with wine; Come, he said, wilt thou always be at thy cups? Give thy stomach a rest from the wine that so bemuses thee. Nay, my lord, said Anna, thou seest an unhappy woman, unburdening her heart in the Lord's presence; there was no wine or strong drink here. (1 Kings 1. 10–15.)

Numerous prayers for help (Samson: Judges, 16. 28; David: 2 Kings 15. 31; Elias: 3 Kings 17. 20) and prayers of thanks (David: 1 Kings 25. 32, 39; 3 Kings 1. 48) are similarly inset in the narratives of the old stories.

These examples suffice. It is clear that the chronological form in which the so-called conflict between people and individual is presented does not correspond to the facts. A second conflict has been detected between worship (*Kultus*) and piety (*Frömmigkeit*). These two activities are supposed to have interfered with each other. This conflict is simply an avatar of the one between Priest and Prophet whose reality we have already questioned. Its inventors seem to delight in turning what is perhaps a useful tension into a fundamental opposition. Liberal protestantism is at the bottom of this view; it dreamed of a purely interior religion and attached it as far as possible to the prophets. Piety, so the story goes, is cramped by ritual. Critics of the ritual of sacrifice make use even of the psalms (especially 49 and 50), which, as a consequence, Duhm (1899) wished to regard as the products of pietists. A great deal of progress has been made since Duhm's time, but the conflict described above remains the working hypothesis of G. Quell's book, *Das kultische Problem der Psalmen* (Stuttgart, 1926). An unprejudiced reading of the psalms is surely enough to resolve it.

The Psalter is Israel's lyrical prayer. We have already heard this people's work-songs, love-songs and battle-songs; God always figured in them, but the psalms are purely religious. Their great characteristic is that they are all, even the least disinterested of them, completely theocentric in outlook. The psalms reflect every stage in Israel's history. Some are very old (e.g. 28, 46, 109) and contemporary criticism attributes a considerable number of them to pre-exilic times. But the post-exilic period also made its contribution; the voice of the *anawim* (poor), for example, democratized the spiritual experience of a man like Jeremias. It does not seem necessary to come as far down as the Machabean age for the most recent compositions—not that this theory can be ruled out of court, for there are psalms in Ben Sirach[3] (second century), and those of the pseudo-Solomon (first century) and Qumran carry on the biblical tradition—but the canon of the Psalter seems to have been closed by the time of the Machabees. The psalms are grouped in collections which existed separately at one time. They were edited and re-edited several times, and this work was probably carried out by men connected with the temple; Mowinckel discerns particularly the hand of the wise men.

The Psalter as we have it today is the book of chants of the second temple, the one rebuilt by Zorobabel between 521 and 515 and finally completed by Herod round about the beginning of the Christian era. Taken as a whole, the Psalter reveals to us the main tendencies of Israel's prayer during those "dark ages". But to a large extent it was a legacy from a past already distant; and as the community, with its new sensibilities, prayed with these ancient texts it emphasized certain aspects of them. It "re-interpreted" them in conformity with the earlier meaning under the guidance of its spiritual directors. It found in them, like the scholar mentioned by

[3] I.e. Ecclesiasticus, written, probably *c.* 185 B.C., by the scribe Jesus Ben Sirach. [*Trans.*]

Jesus (Matt. 13. 52), *nova et vetera* (things new and old). It is safe to assume that every important passage had a life and commentary of its own during the course of its biblical existence. We shall try to convey some idea of this later on.

But it is the complex nature of the Psalter that needs to be especially emphasized. The permanent aspirations of the religious temperament are so well expressed in it that Jesus —*Iste Cantator psalmorum* (that singer of the psalms—St Augustine)—was to find spiritual refreshment in it, and the Christian Church was to preserve and make use of this major legacy of Israel. However, it includes prayers designed for so many different situations that the modern reader receives the impression of a somewhat rich and tangled collection, to which he needs some kind of introduction. H. Gunkel's books (*Die Psalmen*, 1926; *Einleitung in die Psalmen*, 1933) have exerted more influence than any others on contemporary exegesis; no doubt his classifications, like those of Linnaeus, are too rigid, but his efforts to replace the psalms in their context of everyday life have given them back their original vitality and warmth. By classifying them under different "literary forms" he has made it easier to listen to their messages, for the Psalter is the very model of the prayer that opens our hearts. If we re-read each psalm in the spirit in which it was written, we shall gradually notice that we have lent our voice to every kind of prayer, in accordance with St Augustine's advice: "If the psalm prays, pray; if it groans, groan; if it is joyful, rejoice; if it is full of hope, then hope; and if it expresses fear, then feel fear yourself."

Without going into too much detail, I should like to give some idea of the variety to be found in Israel's prayer. To start with, here are the psalms composed for a particular situation. First of all, hymns.

"The Hebrew hymn", says Gunkel, "answers the deepest and noblest need of any religion, that is, to worship in the dust him who is above us. . . . The hymn-writer considers things not from the standpoint of man, rising and falling with the waves, but from the standpoint of God, who can cast down or raise up as he pleases." The hymn helps to mould in the worshipping community that basic religious attitude on which men like Bérulle[4] laid so much emphasis in the seventeenth century: the adoration which "inclines the mind to prostration, wonder, praise, thanks and love" (Olier[5]). The hymn is the lyrical expression of the feeling of God's transcendence, the commentary on, and, as it were, orchestral version of, that attitude of "fear and trembling" that Isaias came to know on the day when he was called (Isaias 6). But this religious respect for the transcendence of God combines with joy, gratitude and love for him who chose Israel. This God was given a complex and almost self-contradictory title: "the Holy One of Israel". So the usual themes of the hymn are Yahweh's dwelling in heaven, the manifestations of his presence in nature, his creation and his providence, God's lofty deeds in history, his blessings and his mercies. And Israel always entertained the conviction that it was impossible to glorify the Lord as he deserved; Ben Sirach's words are a proof of that: "To what end is all our glorifying of him? He, the Almighty, is high above all that he has made. . . . Glorify him as best you may, glory is still lacking, such is the marvel of his greatness" (Ecclus. 43. 30–32).

Hymns accompanied the sacrifice known as a holocaust, in which the victim was entirely consumed by fire; a holocaust was offered up twice every day, morning and evening. Exceptional events in the national life demanded hymns (2 Kings 6. 17) and, above all, so did the three great annual festivals: the Passover, Pentecost and Tabernacles. The lively,

[4] Cardinal Bérulle (1575–1629) was one of the leaders of the great religious revival in France in the first half of the seventeenth century. He founded the French Oratorians. [*Trans.*]

[5] Jean-Jacques Olier (1608–57), a Parisian parish priest, founded the seminary of St Sulpice. [*Trans.*]

popular character of these festivals should be noted; they included processions (Ps. 25. 6; 67. 25 ff; 41. 5), dances (2 Kings 6. 5–14; Ps. 86. 7), prostrations (Ps. 98. 9), gesticulations (Ps. 62. 8; 46. 2; 97. 1), the setting up of flowers and palms (2 Mac. 10. 7). But not everything was spontaneous. Professional guilds interpreted the feelings of the crowd, which sometimes took up a refrain (Ps. 135) and sometimes responded with "amen" (the shout indicating assent to strength), or a sort of cheer, "Hosanna" (Save us!). Sometimes there seems to have been a soloist (Ps. 103; 145). The musical accompaniment was furnished by stringed, wind and percussion instruments (listed in Ps. 150); it was much more impressive than in the Greek sacred lyric, in which the singing was accompanied by the flute.

The hymn was imitated by the prophets, especially by the Deutero-Isaias, the great anonymous writer of the Exile (Isaias 40–55). In his work we even meet a new kind of hymn which may have been influenced by the Babylonian lyric; in it God sings his own praises (Isaias 44. 24–8). The wise men, after the Exile, also imitated the hymns; elements of them are to be found in Job and Ben Sirach. The latter had a particularly lyrical temperament; at the school of wisdom where he taught at the beginning of the second century he used to read to his pupils or colleagues the poems which he wanted to preserve for posterity (Ecclus. 39. 16–35; 42. 15–43. 33). Literary creation is taking place before our eyes. The same is probably true of some of the canticles put into the mouths of biblical characters by the editors of the historical books: those of Daniel and his companions, for example (Dan. 2. 20–3; 3. 26–45, 52–90), Judith (16. 2–18) and Tobias (13). The classical authors put speeches into the mouths of famous men; the biblical writers put psalms. That in itself tells us a good deal about the spirit of Israel.

The hymns, or similar compositions, can be divided into several classes:

1. Praises of Yahweh, emphasizing various different aspects of his power: 8, 18, 28, 32, 64, 67, 99, 102, 103, 104, 110, 112, 113, 114, 116, 134, 135, 144–150.

The structure of these hymns is simple. First comes an invitation to praise Yahweh (*laudate*); then the reason for praising him (*quoniam* or *qui*); and finally a repetition of the initial invitation.

Here, for example, is Psalm 28, which may go back to the ninth century and is called by A. Weiser the *Gloria in excelsis* of the Old Testament. It describes the Lord being praised by the angels for his manifestation in a storm that sweeps through Palestine from north to south. The mountains where pagan gods dwell are shaken; cutting irony is evident in this touch: "The Lord breaks the cedars of Lebanon; bids Lebanon and Sarion leap high as a bullock leaps, breed of the wild ox" (Ps. 28. 5–6).

Later on, the "signs" of God are not always detected where this psalm sees them; the episode of Elias on Sinaï (3 Kings 19) shows that God is more wonderful in the whispering breeze than in the raging tempest. There is a sort of *diminuendo* in the signs, suggesting what Bergson liked to call the humility of God. After the tumult of the theophany, here is the *Et in terra pax*: "And this Lord will give strength to his people; the Lord will give his people his own blessing of peace" (Ps. 28. 11).

But in the Old Testament this "peace" (*shalom*) has the sense of "free expansion" and denotes all the material advantages which God grants to his faithful followers; its overtones, as it were, are blessing, light, life, security, salvation. Fresh overtones are added as Israel gradually acquires a more spiritual conception of religion; in Wisdom 3. 3 peace means entrance into the next world.

2. Praise of Yahweh the King: 46, 92, 95, 98.

These psalms praise an essential attribute of God: his position as lord and master. But this sovereignty is sometimes described as existing now, at others as messianic and eschatological, that is, to become a reality in the last days. The exegesis of these psalms of the Kingdom is therefore a delicate task. Most of them look to the future and celebrate the enthronement of Yahweh as universal king.

Psalm 46 celebrates the ascent of Yahweh, the God of the ark, to Sion, to the sound of horns. It is full of the pride of a strong people. The tribes gather at the sanctuary and are conscious of being Abraham's people. It may be that this psalm celebrates a definite victory, but it seems preferable to see in its nicely-adjusted text an old enthronement-liturgy. Its structure is noteworthy; two invitations frame a brief proclamation:

> Clap your hands, all you tribes, in applause; acclaim your God with cries of rejoicing. The Lord is high above us, and worthy of dread; he is the sovereign ruler of all the land; he has tamed the nations to our will, bowed the Gentiles at our feet, claimed us for his own portion, Jacob the fair, the well beloved.
>
> God goes up, loud are the cries of victory; the Lord goes up, loudly the trumpets peal.
>
> A psalm, a psalm for our God, a psalm, a psalm for our King! God is King of all the land; God sits enthroned in holiness. The rulers of the tribes are gathered, that worship Abraham's God; a God so high, he has the whole land's princes for his vassals. (Ps. 46.)

Interpreted like this, the psalm may date from the early days of the monarchy. At a later date a couple of lines were inserted between verses 8 and 9, introducing, after an additional invitation, the idea of God's universal sway over the pagans (*goyim*): "Sound the hymn of praise! God reigns over the heathen."

This is an excellent example of re-interpretation, which finds support in the text itself. But the re-interpretation enlarges the meaning of the whole of the original text: the word *'eres* which meant Palestine now means the earth, the only area worthy of the Kingdom of God.

We shall meet the psalms of the Kingdom again in the next Chapter, palpitating with Israel's hope.

3. Canticles of Sion: 45, 47, 75 and especially 83, 86, 121 (131).

These pieces celebrate the sanctuary of Yahweh. They were sung on the occasion of pilgrimages, or at special feasts of late origin like the Dedication.[6] Several have an eschatological significance, for Yahweh is one day to reign on Sion (Isaias 2. 1–4).

Psalm 83 is the supreme example of the pilgrim's hymn; his longing for God, his road and his prayer are all described in turn. It seems to have been written for the feast of Tabernacles; the expectation of autumn rain (7) and the royal title given to God (4), point in this direction, at any rate. What is particularly striking is the intimate character the psalmist has succeeded in giving to his fervour. Birds used to come and rest in ancient temples, as they do in our churches. They might come to be regarded as sacred, or just as a nuisance—as in the prologue to Euripides' *Ion*. Here they are humble models to be envied; amid prayers that are usually so virile this Franciscan touch is particularly moving: "Where else should the sparrow find a home, the swallow a nest for her brood, but at thy altar, Lord of hosts, my king and my God?" (83. 4).

Thanksgiving is already expressed in most of these hymns, but there is also a collection of psalms devoted to this subject alone. In some of them we hear the voice of the nation as a whole (66, 123, 128, 135), in others that of particular groups (106, 117) and in others again that of individuals (17, 29, 31, 33, 40, 65, 91, 115, 137).

[6] The anniversary of the purification of the temple by Judas Machabeus in 164 B.C. [*Trans.*]

When people found themselves in a critical position or were about to undertake some difficult enterprise, they would make a vow to God. On the attainment of safety or success, they came to the temple to offer a sacrifice of thanksgiving or *shelem*. The sacrifice consisted of burning part of the victim and eating the remainder (Lev. 22. 17 ff.). This sacred meal, to which friends were invited, was a joyful affair; this is the joy expressed by the wish in Psalms 21. 27 and 68. 33: "Refreshed be your hearts eternally!" This mellow feeling of happiness resulting from Yahweh's blessing and the consciousness of sharing with one's brothers is crystallized in the word *shelem*, which comes from the same root as *shalom*, peace. In biblical phraseology, to have peace means to enjoy an abundance of the material blessings like security, health, life, well-being and light with which God mainly rewards men in the materialistic religion reflected by almost all of the Old Testament. It is not surprising that our old translations speak on these occasions of a "pacific" sacrifice, the word being more or less transliterated from the Hebrew with the shade of meaning defined above. It was called "eucharistic" (i.e. of thanksgiving). To us Christians, who see prefigured in the old Covenant the realities by which we live, it is noteworthy that these sacred meals were a partaking of Yahweh's table, since the food had touched his altar. A psalm known as a *toda*, or thanksgiving, formed the setting for this sacrifice.

Some psalms (65. 13–20; 115. 17–19) seem to postulate a large audience, although they are, in fact, thanksgivings for individual favours. It looks as though individual cases were sometimes grouped together to form a sort of liturgy, which would certainly not be out of place during the octave of the feast of Tabernacles. The harvest had been gathered in and there was time for the performance of such liturgies; the different categories of supplicants can be easily distinguished, for example, in Psalm 106. From every region of the Dispersion, the *hadjis* gathered at Jerusalem. It was like a rehearsal for Pentecost (Acts 2. 9–11). There were caravan-drivers from the desert, freed prisoners, people who had recovered from illnesses, sailors who had escaped the perils of the sea. A real purple passage is devoted to the last-named:

> Some there were that ventured abroad in ships, trafficking over the high seas; these are men that have witnessed the Lord's doings, his wonderful doings amid the deep. At his word the stormy wind rose, churning up its waves; high up towards heaven they were carried, then sank into the trough, with spirits fainting at their peril; see them reeling and staggering to and fro as a drunkard does, all their seamanship forgotten! So they cried out to the Lord in their trouble, and he relieved their distress, stilling the storm into a whisper, till all its waves were quiet. Glad hearts were theirs, when calm fell about them, and he brought them to the haven where they longed to be. Praise they the Lord in his mercies, in his wondrous dealings with mortal men; let them extol his name, where the people gather, glorify him where the elders sit in council. (Ps. 106. 23–32.)

So the whole community joins with these men who have been saved in praising the goodness of God (33–41). There are also *toda* of wider scope in which the voice of Israel as a whole is heard thanking God for a victory, an era of peace or the march of the national history.

This history was not just one long catalogue of successes. It was studded with trials and failures, "dark days" which were ascribed to "the wrath of Yahweh": famines (Jer. 14) and plagues of locusts (Joel 1. 13–15), defeats and oppression (Lam. 1–5). At times like these a fast was proclaimed; it became a regular event on the anniversaries of national disasters (Zach. 8. 19) and at the autumnal Day of Atonement (*Kippur*). The liturgy of national mourning reached its climax when the temple choirs chanted the lamentation in the name of Israel, sometimes protesting its innocence (Ps. 43), at others confessing its sins (Neh. 9).

The lamentation (*qina*) has a fairly well defined structure. The introduction calls on God. In the main body of the poem there are complaints and God is presented with reasons for intervention: his people, his legacy, his sanctuary, his promises are at stake. Key-words keep recurring: "Alas! How long? Remember! Arise." "Forget the long record of our sins, and haste in mercy to our side; never was need so sore as this. O God our Saviour, help us; deliver us, Lord, for the glory of thy name, pardon our sins for the sake of thy own renown!" (Ps. 78. 8–9).

Into this category fall Psalms 43, 57, 73, 78, 79, 82, 105, 122, 124 and 136.

The so-called category of individual complaints offers more difficulties than the previous ones, first because it contains a more varied selection of sub-divisions and second because the question of the original character of these psalms arises. It is difficult to know whether they were written for the liturgy or as spiritual canticles expressing private devotion.

These psalms contain many complaints, and also declarations of innocence, curses, affirmations of confidence and admissions of sin. Numbers 4, 10, 15, 22, 26. 1–6, 61 and 130 are classified by Gunkel as psalms of confidence; 108 as the only psalm expressing nothing but a curse; 6, 37, 50, 68 and 129 as psalms of penitence; 5, 7, 16, 25 as protestations of innocence. A large group remains that looks homogeneous because of the same tone of distress: 3, 12, 21, 24, 26. 6–14, 27, 30, 34, 38, 39. 13–18, 41 and 42 together, 51, 53, 54, 55, 56, 58, 60, 62, 63, 69, 70, 85, 87, 101, 119, 139, 140, 141, 142. But thanksgiving forms part of several of these psalms: 21, 56, 101, 119, for example. H. Schmidt has distinguished a group of psalms for accused persons (3, 4, 5, 7, 10, 12, 16, 25, 26. 1–6, 53, 54, 55, 56, 58, 93, 139 and 141) and another for sick people (24, 27, 34, 37, 40, 68, 85, 101 and 108). On the whole, the boundaries between the different varieties of these individual pleas are not completely rigid. Moreover, they can be interpreted in two different ways.

Many contemporary critics take the view that these psalms were composed for liturgical use. Besides the big public ceremonies there were others which only concerned the individual. A sick person would go to the temple for a liturgy of supplication or expiation, for his disease was the sign of a sin. This private liturgy seems to have consisted of the confession of the sin (Ps. 31. 5), the offering of a sacrifice, other rites like ablutions (Ps. 25. 6–7; 50. 9) and probably a prophecy of recovery or a blessing recited by the officiating priest. It was accompanied, so it is thought, by a psalm, as was the case at Babylon. A number of psalms of lamentation whose details are fairly vague and comprehensive seem applicable to this form of worship; thus the state of mind of every suffering suppliant was sketched in advance. Conversely, in Bentzen's view, some psalms were composed as psalms of thanksgiving with retrospective references to suffering already over. It is obviously difficult to see when we are confronted with psalms of this sort. Psalm 6 might belong to this category; the sudden change of tone noticeable between verses 8 and 9 may leave room for a priestly intervention in the form of a prophecy or blessing, which is a sort of guarantee that the prayer will be heard:

> Lord, when thou dost reprove me, let it not be in anger; when thou dost chastise me, let it not be in displeasure. Lord, pity me; I have no strength left; Lord, heal me; my limbs tremble; my spirits are altogether broken; Lord, wilt thou never be content? Lord, turn back, and grant a wretched soul relief; as thou art ever merciful, save me. When death comes, there is no more remembering thee; none can praise thee in the tomb. I am spent with sighing; every night I lie weeping on my bed, till the tears drench my pillow. Grief has dimmed my eyes, faded their lustre now, so many are the adversaries that surround me.

> Depart from me, all you that traffic in iniquity, the Lord has heard my cry of distress. Here was a prayer divinely heard, a boon divinely granted. All my enemies will be abashed and terrified; taken aback, all in a moment, and put to shame.

Other critics, following Gunkel, think that these psalms belong to a fairly spontaneous form of writing and are to be compared with the "Confessions" of Jeremias. It is well known that this prophet, persecuted and driven far from the temple, took refuge with the God within himself, and poured forth his soul in splendid lyrical monologues inserted by his editor among his oracles (Jer. 11. 18 to 12. 6; 15. 10–21; 17. 12–18; 18. 18–23; 20. 1–7). Obviously Jeremias did not invent the literary form which he uses; he is familiar with the ritual laments discussed above but gives them a fresh spiritual content, of a quality never before attained in Israel:

> Lord, thou hast sent me on a fool's errand; if I played a fool's part, a strength greater than mine overmastered me; morn to night, what a laughing-stock am I, every man's nay-word! Long have I prophesied, and still I clamoured against men's wickedness, and still cried ruin; day in, day out, nothing it earns me, this divine spokesmanship, but reproach and mockery. Did I essay to put the Lord out of my thoughts, and speak no more in his name, all at once it seemed as though a raging fire were locked in my bosom, pierced my whole frame, till I was worn out with it, and could bear no more. (Jer. 20. 7–9.)

The assumption is, then, that psalmists were influenced by the experience of Jeremias, imitated his attitude and phraseology and, as it were, democratized them. P. Bonnard has gone so far as to speak recently of a "psalter according to Jeremias". Whatever hypothesis we accept, these spiritual canticles, originating outside the official ritual, although remotely based on it, became temple property and were finally embodied in its ritual.

If this line of exegesis is accepted, and there is much to be said in its favour, the authors of these psalms are to be sought among the *'anawim* or "poor", who assumed such a large place in the religious life of Israel after the exile. We have attempted elsewhere (*Les pauvres de Yahweh*, Paris, 1953) to sketch the history of this pietistic movement. It is with Sophonias (seventh century) that the vocabulary of poverty begins to express an attitude of mind (Soph. 2. 3; 3. 11–13): poverty (*'anawah*) becomes a willing openness to God, humility before God; the poor man (*'anaw*) comes to be regarded as Yahweh's client. He stakes all on God, even his material security; his faith acquires a tinge of abandonment and becomes a sort of last resort. The exile was a chance to live this ideal as a group, for its circumstances provided the opportunity for a spiritual awakening: the new Israel—with different ideals—began to take shape and was apostrophized thus on the eve of the return to Palestine: "Ring out, heaven, with praise; let earth keep holiday, and its mountains echo that praise again; the Lord brings consolation to *his people*, takes pity on *their need* (or *on his poor*)" (Isaias 49. 13).

Later ages laid emphasis on this equivalence expressed with such bold parallelism (see also Ps. 149. 4); henceforth the "poor" were certain that they formed the true Israel, and were then violently scandalized by the apparently imperfect operation of divine justice: "Who serves God serves him for nothing; what reward is ours for keeping command of his, attending with sad mien the Lord of hosts? Here are proud folk more to be envied than we, ill-doers that yet thrive, abusers of his patience that escape all harm! So they used to talk among themselves, his true worshippers. . . . (Mal. 3. 14–16).

These were the sort of remarks current among the *'anawim*. There was vituperation of those who oozed with the fat of the land and could be happy without being faithful to Yahweh, there were protestations of integrity in vehement and somewhat "pharisaic" language from people who were conscious of forming "the race of the children of God" (Ps. 72. 15). The book of Job expressed in literary form a vast accumulation of experience, but only in order to rise superior to it; its central character no longer has "signs" to which to anchor his religion and no longer receives God's rewards. Losing his property, his health and his reputation is only a beginning; he has lost even the security provided by the accepted theology. This last test was necessary to win his adherence to the omnipotent God, the *Ipsissimus Deus*. Then he is silent with the silence of appeasement. For faith was purified among the *'anawim*; it expressed the vague certainty of the man who persists in saying in the face of every trial: "My God." Thanks to these anonymous persons faith grew deeper, too; the doctrines of grace, the redemption and reward beyond the grave were gradually discovered, brought into view by this personal, trusting relationship with a God who speaks to the heart. The personal experience of the *'anaw* spreads out over the community, for the pious person does not feel isolated, he carries in his imagination the ideal Israel, and even the real Israel, to the very heart of his communion with God. Open to God, he is also open to others, and one day the Greek translation of the Bible was to translate the pregnant term *'anaw*, which Christ applied to himself (Matt. 11. 29), by breaking it up into the two words "gentle and humble". We find this attitude in Ps. 130. The author has lost many illusions but is neither cynical nor downhearted; his very silence is not a form of spiritual pleasure but a sort of brotherly invitation, wishing the new Israel well: "Lord, my heart is not lifted up, my eyes not raised from the earth; my mind does not dwell on high things, on marvels that are beyond my reach. Bear me witness that I kept my soul ever quiet, ever at peace. The thoughts of a child on its mother's breast, a child's thoughts were all my soul knew. Let Israel trust in the Lord, henceforth and for ever."

This basis of communion with God makes the *'anaw* a

mystic, not in the sense of losing himself in God, but because in his case the dialogic structure of religion attains a degree of intimacy resulting from the intensity of reception and response. Rarely has the happiness of this communion been better expressed than in Ps. 15. To make it comprehensible the psalmist refers to the sacred meals terminating sacrificial rites, when the worshipper partook of the "portion" and the "cup". Yahweh can be compared to this sacred food. He can also be compared to that portion of land so dear to every Israelite which holy lot, in those far-off days when Palestine was conquered, assigned to each tribe and its clans. This communion with God never ceases to give strength. It also signifies endless happiness, for love aspires to eternity. At a time when heaven had not yet been revealed, the psalmist seems to have been one of the first to thrill to a hope beyond the tomb. How this hope is to be fulfilled he does not know; he is content to proclaim the power of God over death itself:

> No, it is the Lord I claim for my prize, the Lord who fills my cup; thou, and no other, wilt assure my inheritance to me. Portion is none were more to my liking; welcome the lot's choice. . . . Always I can keep the Lord within sight; always he is at my right hand, to make me stand firm. Glad and merry am I, heart and soul of me. . . . Thou wilt shew me the way of life, make me full of gladness in thy presence; at thy right hand are delights that will endure for ever. (Ps. 15.)

Recently S. Mowinckel[7] drew attention to some psalms of non-ritual origin. The psalms in question are 1, 33, 36, 48, 77, 104, 105, 110, 111 and 126, to which 72 and 118 should perhaps be added. These pieces were written by educated men, scribes, interested in certain questions debated in the schools of wisdom: the fate of the good and the wicked (1, 111), God's provident care of Israel (77, 104, 105), love of the Law (118), the justice of God within the community (33, 36,

[7] "Psalms and Wisdom", in *Wisdom in Israel and in the Ancient Near East*, Leiden, 1955.

48, 72). The sapiential tone of these psalms can hardly be questioned; the problem is to know how they were inserted in a collection of ritual prayers. No doubt most of them were brought to the temple as votive offerings for Yahweh. In ancient Egypt psalms of this sort were engraved on the stones in the courtyards of the sanctuaries; in Israel, with its devotion to the book, they were inserted in the scriptures. These memorials might be useful to future generations; Israel's community-sense and didactic tendency were at work here. Moreover, these sages were themselves *'anawim*, ready to take an educational task seriously. The stanzas of Ps. 118 follow each other like waves: the reader is carried away by the monotonous incantation:

> Idly I strayed till thou didst chasten me; no more shall thy warnings go unheeded. . . . It was in mercy thou didst chasten me, schooling me to thy obedience. . . . Judge me no more; pardon and life for one that loves thy will. . . . Lend me thy aid, for thine I am, and thy bidding is all my quest. . . . My delight, Lord, is in thy biddings; ever my thoughts return to it. . . . (Ps. 118. 67, 71, 77, 94, 97).

The Psalter as a whole provides a picture—a composite work by many hands—of Israel at prayer in the post-exilic age. For it was then, so it seems, that it was finally organized and regularly used in its entirety.

Piety reaches God through a number of "sacraments" of the divine presence. The first is the temple, where his proximity can be apprehended. From it Yahweh speaks (3. 5) and gives his blessing: "May the Lord who dwells in Sion bless thee, the Lord who made heaven and earth!" (Ps. 133. 3). It is the goal of every pilgrim: "O God, my whole soul longs for thee, as a deer for running water; my whole soul thirsts for God, the living God" (Ps. 41. 1–3). And finally, at the temple, one is at the religious centre of the universe: "None was ever born, the proverb shall run, that did not take his birth from her" (Ps. 86. 5).

The community itself is a "sacrament" of God, who lives in it and makes it a place of spiritual expansion. The most personal psalms do not fail to mention this channel of salvation: "Remember me, Lord, with loving thoughts towards thy people, come and strengthen me with thy aid, to witness the prosperity of thy chosen servants, to rejoice with thy people that rejoices, to share the glory of thy own domain" (Ps. 105. 4–5).

God also reveals himself in history; that is why reviews of the past (77, 104, 105, 135) or allusions to the past have such a large place in the Psalter. Yahweh has involved himself in Israel's fate and the signs of his activity stand out clearly: "And now he sent his servant Moses, and Aaron, the man of his choice . . ." (Ps. 104. 26). "In David's reckoning, Lord, let not his patient care be forgotten . . ." (Ps. 131. 1).

This history is not lifeless matter, a frozen past, it is always present to Israel, like a patrimony on which one lives, almost like a mystery into which one is initiated. For Yahweh holds its threads in his hand and gives a hint that his triumphal action of tomorrow will repeat and improve upon his "justice" of days gone by. Thus in Israel the sense of hope was wedded to the sense of tradition, in those celebrations in which the liturgical *Today* formed a bridge between past and future. A new Sinaï lights up before the gaze of the community as it sings: "See where he comes, fire sweeping on before him; burning up his enemies all around. In the flash of his lightning, how shines the world revealed, how earth trembles at the sight! The hills melt like wax at the presence of the Lord" (Ps. 96. 3–5).

For nature, too, expresses the divine power. For God, heaven is both a belvedere and a base for action. "The Lord looks down from heaven" (Ps. 13. 2), but no bound can be fixed to his omnipresence: "Where can I go, then, to take refuge from thy spirit, to hide from thy view? If I should climb up to heaven, thou art there; if I sink down to the world beneath, thou are present still. If I could wing my way eastwards, or find a dwelling beyond the western sea, still would I find thee beckoning to me, thy right hand upholding me . . ." (Ps. 138. 7–10).

God can be apprehended in the noisy manifestations of his transcendence, and we have already seen in the theophanies a simplification of the cosmological proof: "When the glorious God thunders . . ." (Ps. 28. 3).

But in Ps. 103 his daily watchfulness and his immanence in the universe is sung, with a charm and sweetness that give a foretaste of the Sermon on the Mount:

> From thy high dwelling-place thou dost send rain upon the hills; thy hand gives earth all her plenty. Grass must grow for the cattle; for man, too, she must put forth her shoots, if he is to bring corn out from her bosom; if there is to be wine that will rejoice man's heart. . . .
>
> Moisture there must be for the forest tree, for the cedars of Lebanon, trees of the Lord's own planting. . . .
>
> What diversity, Lord, in thy creatures! What wisdom has designed them all! There is nothing on earth but gives proof of thy creative power. (Ps. 103. 13–16; 24.)

But it is in the *Torah* that the faithful follower comes nearest to his God: "The Lord's perfect law, how it brings the soul back to life; the Lord's unchallengeable decrees, how they make the simple learned!" (Ps. 18. 8–9).

Such are the various steps by which one reaches God. There is a key-word in the Psalter, *batah*, which means to believe, to count on, to hope. It implies confidence and security, certainty and joy, nostalgia and self-abandonment. It is, in fact, already the whole complex concept of πίστις (faith) which we find in St Paul.

CHAPTER V

LOOKING FORWARD TO THE KINGDOM OF GOD

All through the Bible we find a hope and an expectation which demand the historian's attention and provide the believer with a solid buttress to his faith. There is a sort of straining towards an ultimate era, an aspiration which coincides with the rhythm of faith. It does not diminish with historical defeats, but is rather galvanized by them into fresh and purer life. Like the torch of progress described by Lucretius, hope is handed on from one generation to the next. It feeds on sublime images which stir men to action by encouraging them to expect and to prepare for the coming of the Kingdom of God. It is believed to be already present, of course, but there remains the aspiration towards an ultimate completeness requiring intervention from on high. Faith clings to this double certainty which gives it its biblical dimensions: salvation is both present and to come. The precise shape of the future was not defined in advance, but some light on it guided humanity in its stumbling advance; men were given a lamp before the dawn broke (2 Peter 1. 19); God spoke through the prophets on many occasions and in many ways (Heb. 1. 1), and if the light he put in their hands sometimes resembled a torch whose light is obscured by smoke, that was part of God's educational method, which is a patient one (Rom. 3. 26).

We have already described how Israel filtered, clarified and spiritualized all man's profoundest experiences since his distant origin. But man was also born to hope, and on the privileged soil of Israel his dreams, too, were rethought, corrected and given a fresh direction.

Humanity hoped, and myths of the golden age are the literary reflection of its dreams. When, in ancient Sumeria, we find descriptions of a perfect land, full of precious metals, where the animals all serve man and there is no disease, old age or death; when, in Phoenician writings, happiness is described in terms of heavenly food ("milk and honey"), we recognize at once that these themes, which occur in the Bible (precious metals: Gen. 2. 10–14, Ezech. 28. 12–13; animals submissive: Isaias 11. 6–8, Ps. 8; milk and honey: Isaias 7. 15; longevity: Isaias 65. 20), are all borrowed from age-old dreams. But these memories were to be re-embodied in a new synthesis.

For Israel's position in the history of humanity is quite unique. The Covenant endowed it with a certain conception of history whose novelty has been well demonstrated by Mircea Eliade.[1]

The God who revealed himself to the patriarchs and Moses is a historical God, that is, a God who supports history and clothes himself in it. The historical dimension is the field of his activity; he intervenes in history to bless or to show his displeasure, and it moves onward at the pace he dictates. History becomes a relationship to God. It has a direction, a meaning and a goal. It is no longer thought of in terms of a continual return; for the image of a closed cycle, which haunted ancient minds, is substituted that of the arrow and the forward leap. History is open to the future, and Israel's optimism springs from its partnership with a God who pursues a plan. The prophets, applying the image of a marriage to Yahweh and his people, were to say that both collaborate in

[1] *Le mythe de l'éternel retour,* Paris, 1950.

a common task: the establishment of the Kingdom of God. The promise to the patriarchs, the leading forth from Egypt, the conquest of Canaan, the establishment of the monarchy and the restoration after the exile were all to be definite stages in the accomplishment of this purpose, a purpose on which Israel was continually called to reflect by the prophets. It saw in it its own peculiar vocation, an invitation to see its future as a continuation of its past and present. It imagined this future as a perfected repetition of its best moments in the past. It transposed to this millennium, which it awaited, elements of its present glory and happiness, whose features gradually became, in Israel's dream, characteristics of the new dispensation. The adjective "new" became the messianic sign and stamp: new golden age, new Covenant, new Jerusalem, new Temple, new man, new heaven and earth, these are the new things to be created one day by the power of God.

For the first time we have used the word messianic. It was desirable to introduce it in its biblical context to make its significance clearer, for it came to be used more and more widely so that its original meaning was considerably enlarged. To start with, the Messias (*mashih*) was the actual king, with particular reference to the ceremony of consecration. To be precise, the Messias was the person anointed with the holy oil (2 Kings 5. 3). The next step was to see on the throne of Israel in the age to come an extraordinary king who should be the descendant of those to whom God had historically entrusted the kingdom of Israel. That was the first form of a complex expectation whose main lines of development we now have to trace.

Let us examine it when it has reached a certain degree of perfection, in the seventh century, an epoch dominated by the figure of the prophet Isaias. The monarchy, to which at the outset David had given such lustre, had been in existence for three centuries. The prophet Nathan, it will be remembered, had come to David in his new capital of Jerusalem, with its ark, Yahweh's mobile sanctuary, to ratify David's success with due solemnity and to proclaim the religious importance of the monarchy:

> So, when thy days are ended, and thou art laid to rest beside thy fathers, I will grant thee for successor a son of thy own body, established firmly on his throne. . . . He shall find in me a father, and I in him a son. If he plays me false, be sure I will punish him; ever for man the rod, ever for Adam's sons the plagues of mortality; but I will not cancel my merciful promise to him. . . . Through the ages, far as thy thought can reach, dynasty and royalty both shall endure; thy throne shall remain for ever unshaken. (2 Kings 7. 12–16.)

What this solemn proclamation means is the regalization, as it were, of the Covenant. Henceforth the Davidic king is to be a party to the Covenant; he is to assume responsibility for it and the duties it entails; he will be a son to God, as was Israel as a whole (Exod. 4. 22); he will concentrate in his person this whole people whose unity he safeguards, and by behaving as moral and religious king he will bring his people earthly success. For, so far as the Old Testament is concerned, the Kingdom of God is to arrive here on earth, and material blessings are always the concomitants and signs of religious values. Grace takes hold of the monarchy, its status is raised, it has a central part to play in the maintenance of the Covenant and becomes one of the central factors in the prospect of salvation.

That is why a number of ancient psalms recited liturgically on behalf or in honour of a king of David's line refer to this charter. Each king knows that he carries within him the future of God's people: "Mine to proclaim the Lord's edict, how he told me, Thou art my son; I have begotten thee this day. Ask thy will of me, and thou shalt have the nations for thy patrimony; the very ends of the world for thy domain" (Ps. 2. 7–8).

The whole dynasty is conscious of a messianic vocation. Every king of David's line knows that the day of his enthronement is also that of his divine adoption. When a new reign begins, the psalmists describe all their expectations of the monarchy, all that it will do one day, sooner or later. They enunciate an ideal, whose content no actual king can exhaust. That is why the old royal psalms look towards the future. Sung for an investiture (Ps. 109; 100; 2; 71), for a birthday (Ps. 20) or a marriage (Ps. 44), at once oracle, complimentary ode and prayer, they remind us of the tasks entrusted to the monarchy and of its promised glory: justice (Ps. 44. 8; 71. 7), religious progress in the world (Ps. 17. 50; 71. 17), peace and fertility (Ps. 71. 7), liberation from the foe (Ps. 20. 9–18) and victorious domination (Ps. 2. 8–12).

But unfortunately as history unrolled it illuminated the kings' inability to fulfil what was expected of them. The prophets were the bold critics of a monarchy unfaithful to its lofty mission, but also the upholders of a hope which grew keener with every crisis and drew irrational comfort from the disappointments of experience.

Isaias, whom we have chosen as a witness, lived through one of these crises. It seemed as though the Jerusalem monarchy was to be carried away like a wisp of straw. King Achaz was unpopular (Isaias 8. 6), Damascus and Samaria had leagued together to put the son of Tabeel on the throne in his place (Isaias 7. 6), the king had wearied God by his lack of faith (Isaias 7. 12), entangled himself in human alliances and sacrificed his eldest son to Moloch (3 Kings 16. 3). The prophet delivers a solemn oracle: the dynasty will continue to exist and the birth of an heir is assured: "Maid shall be with child, and shall bear a son, that shall be called Emmanuel" (Isaias 7. 14).

In a sort of liturgy, Isaias introduces him to the northern provinces as David's successor, but a successor enriched with new and distinctly transcendent qualities. It is the ideal king at last, demanded by the crisis to enable Israel to pursue its destiny:

> For our sakes a child is born, to our race a son is given, whose shoulder will bear the sceptre of princely power. What name shall be given him? Peerless among counsellors, the mighty God, Father of the world to come, the Prince of peace. Ever wider shall his dominion spread, endlessly at peace; he will sit on David's kingly throne, to give it lasting foundations of justice and right; so tenderly he loves us, the Lord of hosts. (Isaias 9. 6–7.)

Isaias was never to give up this vision. A little later, probably at the critical moment when Jerusalem, besieged by Sennacherib (701 B.C.), was, humanly speaking, on the verge of disaster, the memory of David is the basis of the prophet's faith (Isaias 37. 35). He foretells the coming of the Messias, a king of David's line (Isaias 11. 1–4), whom he inserts in a vision of paradise regained: the golden age will return, with peace among the animals, now all vegetarians again and man's willing servants, and even the snake—perhaps an allusion to the powers of evil—harmless to children: "Wolf shall live at peace with lamb, leopard take its ease with kid; calf and lion and sheep in one dwelling-place, with a little child to herd them! Cattle and bears all at pasture, their young ones lying down together, lion eating straw like ox; child new-weaned, fresh from its mother's arms, playing by asp's hole, putting hand in viper's den!" (Isaias 11. 6–8).

And to crown this picture with an explicitly religious touch, which is the express purpose of the passage, we find in verse 9: "Deep as the waters that hide the sea-floor, knowledge of the Lord overspreading the world!"

It will be noticed that in messianic visions religious values do not always occupy the foreground. That is because they are the most difficult to convey in pictures in which the emphasis is on suggestive imagery. But for an Israelite the reference to the "knowledge of God" summed up all the essentials of religion. That is why this verse, together with Jer. 31. 31–34 and Dan. 9. 24, is among the most profoundly spiritual in the Old Testament. One of the aims of Bible-reading should be to trace and isolate these veins of gold.

The expectation of a royal Messias did not always display such a decidedly eschatological trend as we have just observed. Sometimes the belief seems to have been that one day all the monarchs of the dynasty would be kings after God's heart (Jer. 23. 1–4); at other times, that the reigning king was in fact the fulfilment of Israel's hope. Such was the case with the Davidic king Zorobabel in 520 (Agg. 1. 14; Zach. 4. 7–10). But it is fair to say that, in general, expectation was henceforth focused on the Messias to appear in days to come. The clean break in the dynastic succession after Zorobabel probably strengthened the tendency to regard the day of Yahweh and the coming of the Messias as the last chapter in the story of salvation. After the exile, during the "dark ages" of Judaism, this habit of thought took firm root. The old royal psalms were re-interpreted in a new light, and a miraculous Messias awaited. About 320 B.C. an anonymous prophet sang of the Messias' entry into his capital; he gives the scene an archaic look by putting the Messias on the desert sheikh's mount, but he also endows him with new characteristics, above all the humility which characterized the spiritualized religion of the "poor of Yahweh": "Glad news for thee, widowed Sion; cry out for happiness, Jerusalem forlorn! See where thy king comes to greet thee, a trusty deliverer; see how lowly he rides, mounted on an ass, patient colt of patient dam! Chariots of thine, Ephraim, horses of thine, Jerusalem, shall be done away, bow of the warrior be unstrung; peace this king shall impose on the world, reigning from sea to sea, from Euphrates to the world's end" (Zach. 9. 9–10).

But this note of mildness is not the one emphasized by latter-day Judaism. An anonymous prophet raises the stock of David's family by throwing it into the eschatological battle

(Zach. 12. 8, 10, 12; 13. 1). This battle is described as an episode in a myth: ultimate order, like the order which originally emerged from chaos (Ps. 73. 13–17), is the result of a battle in the valleys round Jerusalem between the armies of a universal paganism and the power of Yahweh coming to the help of his people. "We shall be wise to treat all this imagery", says Dodd, "as language suitable for the description of things lying outside the field of normal experience and consequently impossible to convey in simple language." It is none the less a fact that the Messias was placed in this context of battle and glory.

We must now go back to those crucial years of exile (586–538 B.C.) which taught Israel so much. The trial enabled the nation to adopt a fresh orientation. It no longer had a king as mediator or that visible sign of God's presence, the temple. It only had the Scriptures, the priests who commented on them at the synagogue meetings and, above all, the prophets, whom events had proved right. The most perfect example of a prophet had been Jeremias; he had delivered his message not long before the fall of Jerusalem, and the memory of him lingered by the canals of Babylon. Ezechiel and the mysterious Second Isaias (Isaias 40–55) were his spiritual sons, and it was they who planned the new Israel and helped it into existence.

It became aware of the continuity of its history, from Abraham to Moses, from David to Jeremias. This history is a heritage to be exploited, the privileges of the great men of the past are now to be enjoyed by the nation as a whole, all of whose members feel that they are the descendants of Abraham (Isaias 41. 8) and accountable for the graces of David (Isaias 55. 3). Like them, they are witnesses before the nations (Isaias 55. 4), whom they have learnt to know through contacts sometimes cruel (Ps. 136) and sometimes kind (Isaias 44. 5). This rôle is now welcomed in the knowledge that in the past it has been sadly neglected (Ezech. 36. 23); in fact, a new perspective opens, that of Israel as a missionary to humanity at large. The call to proselytize is the particular message of the Second Isaias (Isaias 45. 22–4; 44. 5).

The prophets were not only listened to, but, as it were, discovered. They were the living revelation of a new kind of mediation. They were seen, amid the debris of recent institutions, in the rôle of the earlier mediators, kings or priests. They had taken over the task by being called, like Moses, to assume responsibility for their brothers. Responsible for their brothers, they were concerned for their sins, and interceded for them (Jer. 15. 1); they were answerable to God for the blood of each of them (Ezech. 33. 8), and they symbolically bore the guilt of their people's sins (Ezech. 4. 4–8). This spiritual solidarity was accompanied by loneliness; they were fated not to be understood, and even to be persecuted. There was even a hint of the theology of martyrdom (Jer. 26), which was not to find a clear formulation until the age of the Machabees. But it is already realized that the "word" only takes root through self-sacrifice. The prophets, thus established, form, as it were, Israel's new "structure". That was the soil from which a new form of messianic hope sprang up.

Israel is conscious of being the repository of true religion for the whole world. Perhaps it is this mission which is expressed in what might be described as an oracle of investiture, in which Yahweh speaks:

> And now, here is my servant, to whom I grant protection, the man of my choice, greatly beloved. My spirit rests upon him, and he will proclaim right order among the Gentiles. He will not be contentious or a lover of faction; none shall hear his voice in the streets. He will not snap the staff that is already crushed, or put out the wick that still smoulders; but at last he will establish right order unfailingly. Not with sternness, not with violence; to set up right order on earth, that is his mission. He has a law to give; in the far-off islands men wait for it eagerly. (Isaias 42. 1–4.)

This noble passage is not lacking in prophetic colour. Perhaps Israel was henceforth to be a community that had assimilated the style of the prophets and doctors, and inherited the spirit bestowed on the Messias of Isaias 11. 2. Gradually the figure takes shape. The kings of the earth assemble to lament a character of the future—the Servant of Yahweh—who surpasses any historical figure in dignity and effectiveness. He makes his suffering the means of expiation awaited by a distraught and guilty humanity. It is the figure of a martyr and a Saviour: "Ay, the Lord's will it was, overwhelmed he should be with trouble. His life laid down for guilt's atoning, he shall yet be rewarded; father of a long posterity, instrument of the divine purpose" (Isaias 53. 10).

It is also, although the word is not uttered, the figure of a Messias. For the sublime poem ends with references to victory and the sharing of booty (Isaias 53. 12). This restoration is perhaps already a resurrection.

The portrait of the Servant bore the signature of suffering and humility. The vocabulary of "poverty" was evident in some places (Isaias 53. 4, 7). Soon it would not be difficult to make out at the centre of the age to come the figure of a Poor man (*'anaw*) and that is what Psalm 21 gives us. A "reinterpretation" put side by side the description of the Kingdom of God and an exceptionally detailed picture of this figure, who was thus given a messianic character: "The furthest dwellers on earth will bethink themselves of the Lord, and come back to him; all the races of the heathen will worship before him; to the Lord royalty belongs, the whole world's homage is his due" (Ps. 21. 28–9).

Thus the collaboration of a human person in the renewal of God's kingdom was glorified in an increasingly religious way. The "Servant" is so lofty a figure that he may be said to be in a different and higher class than that of the kings and to replace them. This collaboration between God and a Man to establish the Kingdom conforms in any case to the essential basis of the Covenant, as we have described it. But it must never be forgotten that the Covenant is a grace, that the Kingdom is a gift, that salvation proceeds from God and that Israel, God's partner, is great not because of what it does but because of what it receives. It is probably to enable us to grasp more clearly this fundamental truth that the history of the messianic hope laid fresh emphasis on it.

It is excellently expressed in the Psalms of the Kingdom of Yahweh (Pss. 92, 95–8). It is true that God's eschatological monarchy was awaited even before the exile, and that a passage like Isaias 2. 2–4, without employing the actual title of king, places him on Sion as arbiter of the peoples. But it was in exile that the conception really began to unfold, as it gradually became clear, no doubt, what small efforts the kings of the past had made to live up to their vocation. Would God need human instruments for another epiphany like that of Sinaï? "Thy God has claimed his throne!" is the happy message of the Second Isaias for Sion (Isaias 52. 7–8); the future lies open for God's activities: a new exodus (Isaias 41. 14–20), a new covenant (Isaias 55. 3) and a new canticle (Isaias 42. 10) like Miriam's (Exod. 15. 20–21) are bound up with this message.

It is in fact with a new canticle that the official liturgy, at some post-exilic passover, sings in advance of God's coming (Ps. 97). Not only Israel, but the nations of the earth and the earth itself are invited to rejoice. This joy grows to the noise of trumpets, as in Florent Schmidt's "Psalm 46".[2] The Day of Yahweh is described in advance. The final victory over paganism (vv. 2–3) results in the acclamation of the kingship (v. 6) of Him who comes. This proclamation of God's coming is the most extraordinary feature; it is the nearest approach

[2] A powerful setting of this psalm for soprano, chorus, organ and orchestra written by this modern French composer (1870–1958) in 1904. [*Trans.*]

to the Incarnation: "The sea astir, and all that the sea holds, the world astir, and all that dwell on it; the rivers echoing their applause, the hills, too, rejoicing to see the Lord come. He comes to judge the earth; brings the world justice, to every race of men its due award" (Ps. 97. 7–9).

A new but related messianic theme is that of the "Son of Man" (Dan. 7). Here we are on apocalyptic ground and the writing dates from the second century before Christ. A scene set in heaven shows us God proceeding to a solemn investiture. The person invested is described as "a Son of Man" advancing on the clouds. This is a common mode of transport for heavenly beings in Semitic thought, and it passed into the Bible (Isaias 19. 1; Ps. 67. 5). We are dealing here with a sort of celestial parallel, a visionary duplicate of the new spiritual Israel, which is described as "the people of the most high God" (Dan. 7. 18, 22, 25, 27). The "Remnant" is the recipient, then, of promotion conferred from on high and therefore of an entirely fresh kind. The holy people is to receive the kingdom as a supernatural gift:

> Then I saw in my dream, how one was riding on the clouds of heaven, that was yet a son of man; came to where the judge sat, crowned with age, and was ushered into his presence. With that, power was given him, and glory, and sovereignty; obey him all must, men of every race and tribe and tongue; such a reign as his lasts for ever, such power as his the ages cannot diminish. (Dan. 7. 13–14.)

This very important passage, whose primary meaning, dictated by the correspondence of verses 14 and 27, we have tried to give, may possibly envisage, connected with the people of Israel and summing it up, a heavenly leader possessing the qualities, if not the name, of a Messias. As the pagan kingdoms, whose fate is described in the same chapter, are represented, according to the reading attested by the Hebrew text (v. 17), by their kings, it seems reasonable to see the holy people personified in a leader. In any case, that was the reading adopted by the apocalyptic tradition and, above all, by Jesus himself. By presenting himself as "the Son of Man", particularly at the most solemn moment in his ministry, before Caiphas and the Sanhedrin (Mark 14. 61–2), Jesus wished to identify himself with a transcendent figure, of celestial origin, entrusted with a mission of judgement and salvation. He thus expressly associated himself with an apocalyptic current of thought almost unknown to the Jewish Bible but well fitted, in his view, to express something of his own mystery.

All we have done is to give a bird's eye view of the intricacies of a particularly complex expectation. We shall have more to say of Israel's hopes in the next two chapters as well. This one has at any rate suggested a general picture of the Kingdom of God. Fresh details and colours were continually being added to it, for the historical and the eschatological, the material and the spiritual, the human and the divine all entered into this unique and multiple theme which formed the subject of Israel's dreams from the time of the Covenant onwards. The story of salvation, it was felt, would reach a final climax. The Jewish theocracy would achieve victory (Pss. 2, 109) and universal domination (Ps. 71. 8–11); Jerusalem would enjoy glory in the midst of her vassals (Isaias 60. 5–6, 10, 16); the Holy Land would be transformed (Ezech. 47) and luxuriant (Ps. 71. 16); its inhabitants would all live to the age of a hundred (Isaias 65. 20); death would be abolished (Isaias 25. 8). All this splendour would merely be the setting for more important realities. Justice and peace would be established (Isaias 9. 16); the "knowledge of the Lord" (Isaias 11. 9; Hab. 2. 14) would be facilitated by the granting of a new Covenant (Jer. 31. 31–4); the new people would fulfil all the demands of morality with the help of grace (Ezech. 36. 25–8); the worship of the Lord would be perfect (Zach. 14); the Law would be the light of the world (Isaias 2. 3; Wisdom 18. 4); religious universalism would become a fact (Isaias 19. 23–5); Jerusalem, the religious metropolis of the world, would be inhabited by the "poor of Yahweh" (Soph. 11–13) and within its walls would be fulfilled the purest dream imagined by the Old Testament: "It is ordained that this people of thine, that holy city of thine, should wait seventy weeks before guilt is done away, sin ended, wrong righted; before God's everlasting favour is restored, and the visions and the prophecies come true, and he who is all holiness receives his anointing" (Dan. 9. 24).

CHAPTER VI

THE MISSIONARY IDEAL

The reader will no doubt have noticed, in the preceding chapter, the precise moment when Israel became aware of its missionary function. He may also have taken the view that this moment arrived rather late for, in our definition of the Covenant, we said that it implied positive action by the human partner in conjunction with the divine Partner to establish the Kingdom of God, and this Kingdom concerns all mankind.

That is quite true, but we must never forget that the Bible is the story of a journey. In it, ideas are not presented with the clarity of deductions; they emerge as the fruit of experience, slowly but surely. It has sometimes been asked—rather unwisely—why the Revelation was not entrusted to a people endowed with richer intellectual gifts. The answer may be that God preferred this gradual advance to a rigorously logical demonstration. Israel offers us, not well constructed theses, but the experiences it had and the discoveries it made under the guiding hand of God.

It is a fact that, from the beginning, God's plan covers the whole of mankind. The first historical synthesis in the Bible, the Yahwist document, presents us from the start with clearly universalist views. Adam appears in it as a character, but he is also more than a character: he is the root of humanity. We have in him a real symbol for the whole of mankind. In

Adam are affirmed its unity, its appeal for salvation, its fellowship in sin and also in the promise. For it is at the departure from Paradise that God says to the Serpent: "And I will establish a feud between thee and the woman, between thy offspring and hers" (Gen. 3. 15).

Against this solid and ever-present background the Yahwist tells the story of the call of Abraham. God declares to the man he has chosen: "In thee all the races of the world shall find a blessing" (Gen. 12. 3). The sacred writer looks towards the future and says in effect: the end will correspond to the beginning; the unity symbolized by Abraham will be restored by means of the chosen people. This universalist proclamation does not yet imply a missionary duty for Abraham, that is, human participation in the task of converting the "races of the world". But it does at any rate show that the Election is presented in the same ecumenical terms as those employed by the Yahwist in his catalogue of the nations, who are described as all springing from the same root (Gen. 10). God does not forget mankind: "The Ruler of all has divided the nations apart, sundering Adam's children and giving to each people its own home, peoples as numerous as the sons that sprang from Israel; but one was the Lord's treasured possession, his own people; it was Jacob he had marked out for his own domain."

The nations are provided with protectors, identified by Deut. 4. 19 with the stars and regarded as angels, but Yahweh has reserved Israel for himself and the personal tuition of the Covenant: "Nation is none I have claimed for my own, save you" (Amos 3. 2).

But Israel does not turn its back on the other nations. We meet its great capacity for giving a sympathetic welcome to others even in the prophet Ezechiel, who at first sight seems insensitive to this tendency, since he was to guide Judaism into a policy of withdrawal. When Ezechiel is looking for irreproachable examples of morality he turns to three men outside Israel: Noah, who saved his family from the flood, Daniel, that just king who appears in Phoenician texts—he saved his children—and finally Job the Edomite, whose story has been preserved in the Bible (Ezech. 14). We have already seen how, in Israel's history, this talent for welcoming and absorbing others came to terms with the necessity for careful selection. But we are still a long way from the missionary attitude.

We are no closer to it when we turn to what might be described as Israel's normal policy of recruitment and integration. When the people of Israel waged a war, it took prisoners, particularly female prisoners, for the anathema or ban often required the slaughter of the men (see the case of the fair captive in Deut. 21. 10–14). There can be no doubt that these people adopted the religious practices of Israel. Marriages with female prisoners and foreign women raised the numbers of Yahweh's followers. "Thy God shall be my God," said Ruth the Moabite to her mother-in-law (Ruth 1. 16). The absorption of the peoples of Canaan was a gradual process; metics (*gerim*), that is, foreigners living in Israel, became second-class Israelites, but Israelites all the same. No hint of racialism is apparent in 1 Par. 2. 34, which mentions an Israelite father who gave his daughter in marriage to his Egyptian servant. It looks as though David pursued an active policy of amalgamation and, according to Deut. 23. 7–9, Edomite and Egyptian can be allowed to join Israel.

But after noting this readiness on Israel's part to welcome other peoples into its ranks we must also realize that there were limits to it. "The legislator", writes the pseudo-Aristaeus in the second century before Christ (he is referring to Moses), "enclosed us in inviolable barriers and walls of iron, to prevent us mixing in any way with any other nation." The Israelite community, that band of brothers depicted in Deuteronomy, had its own laws of internal cohesion; its very stability and sense of fellowship were the outcome of a certain degree of isolation. The Covenant was a discipline and, to use Hempel's term, an *Abgrenzung* (marking off, separation); the Israelite had to defend his spiritual integrity. Separation from the pagans and spiritual concentration were the consequence of a difficult vocation. It is well known that this attitude sometimes tended to harden into introspection, pride, an exaggerated national consciousness, contempt for other nations and unsociability (*ἀμιξία*). Tacitus bluntly attributes to the Jews "hostility and hatred for all other people" (*adversus omnes alios hostile odium*—Hist. V. 4).

T. Preiss quite rightly said: "By its exclusive attitude, Israel kept alive the faith of the prophets", and he added this apparent paradox: "It was by its exclusive attitude that it preserved its missionary force." In other words, by remaining true to itself it retained its power of attraction, before disclosing, when the right moment arrived, a great capacity for propagation.

Israel, then, as a people, is God's witness, drawing on itself the eyes and attention of the world. In a pregnant, if slightly ambiguous phrase, E. Jacob pointed out that at a certain period "the mission was only centripetal". "It is no false God that Jacob worships, no senseless image that has its shrine in Israel; the Lord dwells with them as their God; his royal trumpets sound for victory" (Num. 23. 21).

That should be Israel's normal state. Then the nations, whose mouthpiece Balaam is in this passage, can say: this is Yahweh's people; Yahweh's plan is successful. The little Psalm 66, read in this light, is particularly suggestive:

> May God be merciful to us, and bless us; may he grant us the favour of his smile. Make known thy will, O God, wide as earth; make known among all nations thy saving power. . . . Honour to thee, O God, from the nations, honour from all the nations! The land has yielded its harvest; such bounty God,

our own God, affords. God grant us ever his blessing, and may earth, far and wide, do him reverence (Ps. 66. 1–3, 6–8).

If a king can say, in a similar tone, "Then, Lord, I will give thee thanks in the hearing of all nations, singing in praise of thy name", it is because he refers to victories which are the mark of God, as it were, on his people. Israel bears witness to God by the mere fact of its successful existence. This leads to the question, what happens when Israel runs into serious difficulties, as it did from the time of the Assyrian empire onwards?

It is true that the set-back can be explained as the result of Israel's sins, in conformity with the principle laid down by Amos: "Nation is none I have claimed for my own, save you; and guilt of yours is none that shall go unpunished" (Amos 3. 2).

However, by engineering what is, in human terms, a reverse, Yahweh performs a deed that is, as it were, double-edged. In the normal course of events it would be bound to damage his own reputation as well. For in so far as Israel was a sign from God, it has clouded the glory of God before the nations. Ezechiel's slogan was one day to be: "You profane my name in the midst of the nations." But in the event the reaction to the continuous decline in Israel's fortunes was the realization that this was just the moment to invoke the name of the Lord. Let Sion grow powerful and even become the centre of the world! This dream, this expectation is expressed in Isaias' great prophecy, which reflects an admirable aspiration fittingly to fill the rôle of witness:

> In later days, the mountain where the Lord dwells will be lifted high above the mountain tops, looking down over the hills, and all nations will flock there together. A multitude of people will make their way to it, crying, Come, let us climb to the Lord's mountain-peak, to the house where the God of Jacob dwells; he shall teach us the right way, we will walk in the paths he has chosen. The Lord's commands will go out

from Sion, his word from Jerusalem, and he will sit in judgement on the nations, giving his award to a multitude of peoples. They will melt down their swords into plough-shares, their spears into pruning-hooks, nation levying war against nation and training itself for battle no longer. (Isaias 2. 2–4.)

This idea of the conversion of the world inspires one of the pre-exilic prophets: "And after that, all the peoples of the world shall have pure lips, invoking one and all the Lord's name, straining at a single yoke in the Lord's service" (Soph. 3. 9).

So the people of Israel was to develop from witness into missionary. This decisive step may be regarded as the particular grace of the exile, which was a turning-point for Israel. No state or religious centre existed any longer; only the Scriptures, by which Israel always bears witness, as the Second Isaias was to point out (Isaias 42. 9; 43. 10 ff.; 44. 6 ff.). It was also a turning-point in the sense that Israel mixed more thoroughly with the other peoples of the east, discovered other nations with their virtues and failings, and conversed with them on familiar terms.

Israel began to study its vocation more deeply. It was reinterpreted through the great figures of the nation's past: Abraham, who himself was apparently of no account among the pagans and yet was the standard-bearer of monotheism; David, who praised the greatness of God before kings (Isaias 55. 4; *cf.* 17. 50); and finally Moses, who was the principal actor before an audience of Egyptians in that ancient exploit of Yahweh's, the Exodus. History was going to repeat itself, for this reason: Yahweh himself was, as it were, forced to a decision; he had to act in order to avoid abdicating his glory to other gods, to idols (Isaias 42. 8). And Israel's rôle was to be that of leading the Gentiles to recognize Yahweh's glory, which would be made manifest when he miraculously restored his people to its own land, as in days gone by.

There would be real amazement among the Gentiles, and that would be the starting-point for their conversion. They would be converted by this divine intervention, which was to be immediately exploited by proselytizing. It is the first time in the Bible that we hear the phraseology of religious propaganda: "Turn back to me, and win deliverance, all you that dwell in the remotest corners of the earth; I am God, there is no other. By my own honour I have sworn it, nor shall it echo in vain, this faithful promise I have made, that every knee shall bow before me, and every tongue swear by my name. Then shall men say of the Lord, that redress and dominion come from him" (Isaias 45. 22–5).

There we have a glimpse of missionary enthusiasm. The vision is intensified when the author, staring harder into the future, sees this preaching continued by the Servant of Yahweh: "He will proclaim right order among the Gentiles" (Isaias 42. 1). "I have appointed thee to be the light of the Gentiles, in thee I will send out my salvation to the furthest corners of the earth" (Isaias 49. 6).

He will also suffer martyrdom:

> No stateliness here, no majesty, no beauty, as we gaze upon him, to win our hearts. Nay, here is one despised, left out of all human reckoning; bowed with misery, and no stranger to weakness; how should we recognize that face? How should we take any account of him, a man so despised? Our weakness, and it was he who carried the weight of it, our miseries, and it was he who bore them . . . and all the while it was for our sins he was wounded, it was guilt of ours crushed him down; on him the punishment fell that brought us peace, by his bruises we were healed. Strayed sheep all of us, each following our own path; and God laid on his shoulders our guilt, the guilt of us all. (Isaias 53. 2–6.)

> His life laid down for guilt's atoning, he shall yet be rewarded: father of a long posterity, instrument of the divine purpose. (Isaias 53. 10.)

But this missionary charter was not to mean unhindered progress. Such a new movement had to come to terms with all the resentment accumulated against Babylon and Edom (Ps. 136. 7–9). A subordinate status within God's people is often envisaged for the converted *Goyim*; shortly after the return from exile a prophet finds this prospect enchanting: "Strangers they shall be that tend your flocks for you, farm and vineyard alien hands shall till; for you, a higher name, a greater calling, priests and chosen ministers of the Lord our God. All the wealth of the nations shall be yours to enjoy, their spoils shall be your boast" (Isaias 61. 5–6).

Some time later Esdras' matrimonial policy (1 Esdras 9–10) displays a racial tendency; Israel's true character had to be preserved by drastic measures. These advances and retreats will not shock those who have realized that, in Israel, ideas progress in a dialectical fashion, by advances in alternate directions. Israel was to hesitate between sectarian tendencies and ecumenical aspirations. J. Bonsirven wonders whether, round about the Christian era, the Jewish religion, by identifying itself with the Jewish nation, did not burden itself with a weight liable to crush it.[1] In fact, Bonsirven continues, this weight did not crush the Jewish religion to the extent of stifling and destroying it, but it did force it down so firmly into a national framework that it was unable to blossom out and expand. H. H. Rowley has suggested[2] that the great mistake of Judaism was that it remained static and refused to follow the guidance of the Holy Spirit beyond the very high point it had already reached. This reflection provides an invitation to examine this very high point attained in the pre-Christian "Dark Ages".

[1] J. Bonsirven, *Les idées juives au temps de Notre Seigneur*, Paris, 1934, p. 84.

[2] H. H. Rowley, *The Missionary Message of the Old Testament*, London, 1955, p. 79.

The legacy of the Second Isaias can be traced in the prophet Zacharias, who proclaims, soon after the return from exile:

> What alien throngs, from what far cities, shall make pilgrimage yet! And ever, as fresh towns they reach, says pilgrim, Come with us, and welcome; court we the divine favour, to the Lord of hosts repair we; says townsman, Go with you I will. No nation so populous, no kingdom so strong, but shall betake itself to Jerusalem, to find the Lord of hosts and court his divine favour. This, too: A time is coming, when there is never a man of Jewish blood but shall have ten Gentiles at his heels, and no two of the same speech; clinging all at once to the skirts of him, and crying, Your way is ours! The tale has reached us, how God is there to protect you. (Zach. 8. 20–3.)

Such passages are not uncommon. In the liturgies which sing in advance of Yahweh's kingdom we can surely hear an enthusiastic appeal for the conversion of the Gentiles, a sort of orchestral version of themes from the Second Isaias: "Tribes of the heathen, make your offering to the Lord, an offering to the Lord of glory and homage, an offering of glory to the Lord's name; bring sacrifice, come into his courts, worship the Lord in holy array. Before the Lord's presence let the whole earth bow in reverence; tell the heathen, The Lord is king now . . ." (Ps. 95. 7–10).

The Chronicler,[3] too, finds occasion to show us that the pagans are at home in the temple of Jerusalem:

> Nay, is it some stranger, with no part in thy people Israel, who yet comes here from distant lands, for love of thy renown, for the constraining force thy power displays, and worships thee in this temple? Still, in heaven, thy secure dwelling-place, thou wilt grant the alien's prayer. So shall all the world come to hear of thy renown, and fear thee no less than Israel itself; shall doubt no more that this temple I have built claims thy protection. (2 Par. 6. 32–3.)

As well as the liturgy and echoes from the temple, an even bolder voice makes itself heard, suggesting that it is not

[3] I.e. the author of Paralipomenon (Chronicles). [*Trans.*]

enough to wait for the pagans—that had been more or less the position since the Second Isaias—but that they must be sought out and the word of God carried beyond the walls of Jerusalem, right to Nineveh. The book of Jonas is no less than a manual for missionaries. The story it tells is too well known to need repetition here. The whole narrative is shot through with humour, which is a sign of health and possibly a substitute for emotion. Jonas, the hero of the tale, bears a name, chosen on purpose, which means "pigeon" or, in other words, "stay-at-home". This prophet who does not want to venture abroad is called by God to make a missionary journey to the east. As he is pig-headed and prophets do sometimes resist divine invitations, he starts off for the west, in the direction of Spain. After many an adventure God brings him back to his starting-point. But his troubles are not over yet: God sends him on a missionary journey to Nineveh. At the time when the book was written Nineveh had long ceased to exist. It is a symbolic city, of inordinate size. As a centre of paganism, it has to be huge. It might almost be described as a Babylon, but a Babylon full of interesting people, depicted with considerable sympathy. Yahweh could not fail to be interested in them. Jonas still feels bitter, but he does his job as a preacher, and Nineveh is converted. Jonas or the successful missionary: it is not so much an incident that really happened as a stimulus to action. The definition of God to be found in Exodus 34. 6–7 appears again here on the lips of the missionary: "I knew from the first what manner of God thou art, how kind and merciful, how slow to punish, how rich in pardon . . ." (Jonas 4. 2). This almost racialist attitude has been mentioned here because it symbolizes the resistance of certain Jewish circles, whose criticisms can easily be imagined. But, as St Jerome notes in his commentary, "the great and fair city of Nineveh prefigures the Church. . . ." Missionary activity is in the air. There is more contact between the inhabitants of different countries, and a passage of late origin inserted in the book of Isaias describes how Israel will become a blessing to the earth, in accordance with the old promise to Abraham (Gen. 12. 3):

> There will be a high-road, then, between Egypt and the Assyrians; either shall visit other, and Egypt and Assyria be at peace. And with these a third people shall be matched; who but Israel, source of the whole world's happiness? Such blessing the Lord of hosts has pronounced upon it, Blessed be my people in Egypt, and the home I have made for the Assyrian to dwell in; but Israel is the land of my choice. (Isaias 19. 23–5.)

We are gradually arriving at the climax of the Dispersion. The Diaspora, it will be recalled, meant the expansion of the Jews all over the Near East and around the Mediterranean, wherever the olive-tree grows. It put Jews into contact with people whom they worked hard to bring into the synagogues. They preached and were sometimes martyred. The martyrs of the book of Daniel give quite a good picture of Jews who are not afraid to bear witness before kings. The debates to be found in the same book, those conversations with Nebuchadnezzar, reflect fairly accurately Jewish sermons, too. These Jews of the Dispersion assimilated Greek culture and handed on the message of the Bible in the language of their adopted countries. The Bible, translated into Greek, was an excellent instrument of propaganda. The one God was preached as opposed to a multiplicity of gods, the holy God as opposed to the often dubious morality of the legends about these gods. The Bible rationalized monotheism, so to speak, by giving God for the first time a universal name instead of a private one. In the world of the Diaspora the ritual of Judaism lost its importance. The sacrifice became more of an interior sacrifice. The messianic texts made clearer for other nations the element of expectation which they contained. In the Dispersion, moving appeals for the conversion of Hellas make themselves heard:

> O Hellas, why do you trust in men, in mortal leaders who cannot escape the death that awaits them? Why do you make

vain offerings to the dead, why do you sacrifice to idols? What has inspired you to commit such errors in the face of almighty God? Revere the name of the Father of all things; let his name no longer be unknown to you. When the anger of almighty God falls on you, then you will know the face of almighty God. O unhappy Hellas, give up your proud thoughts, pray to the magnanimous and eternal God, control your presumptuous pride, venerate almighty God, so as to share Israel's happy lot.

That quotation comes from the Sibylline oracles.[4] We still possess a huge missionary literature which bears witness to the efforts of Judaism. A specialist, Dalbert, has analysed a dozen books belonging to it. So Judaism was, in the words of J. Jeremias, "the first great missionary religion of the Mediterranean world".

[4] The Sibylline oracles (not to be confused with the original Sibylline Books of Rome, destroyed in the burning of the Capitol in 83 B.C.) are Judaeo-Hellenic and Judaeo-Christian works. They consist mainly of warnings and prophecies of catastrophe; the oldest probably date from the second century before Christ. [*Trans.*]

CHAPTER VII

THE YEARNING FOR A LIFE AFTER DEATH

"Death, too, shall be engulfed for ever" (Isaias 25. 8). This cry from an anonymous commentator comes fairly late in the development of Israel's religion. It does at least bring a clear and decisive answer to a problem of which the Jews had always been obscurely conscious, even if it had not always worried them very acutely. About the same time the Stoic and Epicurean philosophers were trying to solve this problem of death by the exercise of reason; in their view the essential thing was to shed an irrational fear. They were content to deny the more mysterious aspects of a fate which man was invited to meet with nothing more than his own courage and clarity of thought. The Jew, on the contrary, faithful to his usual attitude, appealed to Yahweh, whose omnipotence would finally eliminate the scandal of death.

This affirmation of faith gradually became more and more explicit. But before we follow this development it will be as well to recall what the world of the dead meant for Israel.

As far back as we can trace, Israel adopted a paradoxical attitude before the fact of death. The dead were regarded simultaneously as poor creatures, dependent on the mercy of the living, and as beings endowed with superior knowledge and superhuman power, who were to be feared and conciliated. This ambivalent attitude has a very ancient origin, which need not be discussed here, since we are not concerned with the prehistory of Jewish attitudes and ideas. It is enough to emphasize that in this point, as in so many others, the chosen people took over a human legacy and developed it with the grace conferred by the Covenant. For man had long believed in the mysterious survival of the dead; this belief is at the root of both ancestor-worship—necromancy—and the pains taken to furnish burials with useful objects.

In the Bible this survival is generally conceived in the most neutral terms imaginable: the dead are only shadows, pale editions of the living. A brief incursion into anthropology will help us to form a clearer picture of this attenuated state. When the Hebrew speaks of man, he has in mind the concrete, living person that he calls the *nefesh* (Gen. 2. 7; 12. 5; Lev. 7. 20–1; Lam. 3. 25); in Psalm 102. 1, "*ma nefesh*" could well be translated by "my being", and in many passages it is a slightly emotional equivalent of the reflexive pronoun "myself" (1 Kings 18. 1; Job 30. 25). It can never be grasped apart from the flesh (*basar*) which is its manifestation. The Hebrew always puts before us a synthetic psycho-physiological organism whose various constituent elements can acquire a lofty significance; in a large number of passages the face, the eye, the hand, the bones and the blood all seem to concentrate and sum up its vital force. But this vital force is only lent to it from on high. It experiences fluctuations. It has to be renewed and recharged, as it were, with *rouah* (breath, spirit); in this way God restores the always unstable equilibrium which he created in the beginning (Gen. 2. 7). At the moment of death the *nefesh* is almost completely run down and the dead are more or less totally devoid of vital energy. But they are not destroyed. The concept of *nefesh*, imperfect and vague as it was, formed a means of safeguarding the persistence of the personality. In short, death is conceived, to use E. Jacob's words, "as a state in which the life-force is at its lowest ebb". The dead are feeble creatures, *refaïm* (from a root which means "to be flabby"), and the place reserved for them under the earth, the *sheol* (according to Albright the word is equivalent to the Babylonian *shuaru*, the kingdom of the dead), is well adapted to their wretched state. People are afraid to go to this place of darkness (Ps. 87. 13; Job 10. 21–2) and silence (Ps. 93. 17), a real prison with formidable gates, for the life there is dismal and lethargic: "There will be no doing, no scheming, no wisdom or skill left to thee in the grave (*sheol*), that shall soon be thy home" (Eccles. 9. 10). The just and the sinful rub shoulders in this "home . . . appointed for all living men" (Job 30. 23). If there is any inequality in this world of the dead, it is not due to their virtues or sins, but is apparently a relic of their previous social position or a result of their uncircumcised state (Ezech. 32. 18 ff.; Isaias 14. 9, 18 ff.). The *sheol* is not a place where men are rewarded; the only rewards originally envisaged by the religion of the Old Testament were the earthly blessings bestowed by Yahweh.

The Bible lays considerable emphasis, then, on the drabness of the *sheol* and on the impotence of the dead. If we are to believe W. Oesterley, there is a purpose in this emphasis. For there is another aspect of this strange world which the Bible has not entirely succeeded in hiding. It cannot say much about it without incurring the charge of inconsistency. When the witch of Endor, at the request of Saul, conjures up the spirit of Samuel (1 Kings 28. 13), what she sees rising from the ground is an *elohim* (supernatural being). The scene is reminiscent, in its dramatic intensity, of the evocation of Darius in Aeschylus' *Persae*. The Law sternly opposed these attempts at communication, but Martin-Achard considers that the frequent repetition of this veto reveals how ineffective it was (Lev. 19. 31; 20. 6, 27; Deut. 18. 11). Moreover, the term *refaïm* is not altogether free from ambiguity; according to the Phoenician texts from Ras Shamra, it was applied to divine beings connected with Baal, whose job it was, in the fertility legends, to descend into hell in order to replenish from there the productive energy of the earth. According to R. Gordis, the word could be connected with the root *rafa*, which expresses the two contradictory ideas of weakness and strength. Mourning customs, too, show evidence of opposing attitudes and intentions: pious respect for the dead, but also anxiety to be protected from them or to win their favour.

Finally, some emphasis must be laid on what Martin-Achard describes as the "dynamic" character of the *sheol*. Death, Chaos, Ocean and Darkness all constitute active forces; the kingdom of the dead is regarded as the *Abaddon* (Destruction—Job 26. 5–6; Ps. 87. 12; Prov. 15. 11). They are all obscure, related forces continually threatening God's creation. There is more than mere poetry in the passages describing this aggressive activity: "All about me surged the waves of death, deep flowed the perilous tide, to daunt me; the grave had caught me in its toils, deadly snares had trapped my feet" (Ps. 17. 5–6).

Death encroaches on God's domain and finally causes separation from God. Elegies for the dead do not normally mention Yahweh's name; this is clear from the masterpiece of this kind of writing, David's lament over Saul and Jonathan (2 Kings 1. 17–27). Death prevents all religious activity, and one is moved in advance by this prospect of separation:

> Thou hast no praise in the world beneath, death cannot honour thee; those who go down into the grave have no promise of thine to hope for. . . . (Isaias 38. 18.)

> Not for the dead thy wonderful prayer is shewn; not for pale shadows to return and give thee thanks. There in the grave, how shall they recount thy mercies; how shall they tell of thy faithfulness, now that life is gone? How can there be talk of thy marvels in a world of darkness, of thy favour in a land where all is forgotten? (Ps. 87. 11–13.)

> I count as one of those who go down into the abyss, like one powerless. As well lie among the dead, men laid low in the grave, men thou rememberest no longer, cast away, now, from thy protecting hand. (Ps. 87. 5–6.)

These long preliminaries have at last brought us back to the question posed at the beginning of this chapter: is Death to have the last word? As the theme of this series would suggest, the answer is to be found in the hearts of believers, and it is the answer of faith and hope.

This faith and this hope are based on the God of the Covenant, the starting-point of all biblical thinking about God. Yahweh chose a people, involved himself in its historical development and displayed his power in blessings as well as punishments: "Now you shall learn that I alone am God; there are no others to rival me; it is mine to kill and to quicken, mine to smite and to heal; from my power there is no deliverance" (Deut. 32. 39).

This providential care of Israel resulted, after various trials and set-backs, in the emergence of a people differing from others more and more in spiritual quality, a Remnant whose first educators were the prophets. God's people felt certain that its history had a meaning; and the messianic dream crystallized this vague feeling into a definite expectation. The essential thing was to abide loyally by the terms of the Covenant; that was the key to survival. "Make it your first care to find the kingdom of God, and all these things shall be yours without the asking" (Luke 12. 31). The purpose of the prophets' warnings was to keep fresh the theme of conversion, which would give new life to Israel: "Ay, in their distress they will be waiting full early at my door; Back to the Lord! will be their cry; salve he only can bring, that wounded us; hand that smote us shall heal. Dead men today and tomorrow, on the third day he will raise us up again, to live in his presence anew" (Osee 6. 1–3).

Obviously this passage is only speaking of a symbolic resurrection. The people has been smitten by some scourge and is compared to a sick person. But by the time we come to the Exile, Ezechiel is comparing Israel to warriors who have died in battle (Ezech. 37); Yahweh will repeat for their benefit the miracle of creation (Gen. 2. 7); the spirit (*rouah*) will enter their corpses and bring them to life again (Ezech. 37. 10). This is a promise of national restoration, but it is made in realistic terms which suggest that the idea of the resurrection of the dead was in the air. This idea may also lie beneath the surface of the great poem of the Servant (Isaias 52. 13–53). We have already met this eschatological figure of a prophet-martyr, who by his teaching and sufferings is to establish the kingdom of Yahweh. His execution will be followed by his rehabilitation; this is described in vague terms which leave the impression that the writer is alluding to an indescribable event whose precise nature he cannot define: "His life laid down for guilt's atoning, he shall yet be rewarded; father of a long posterity, instrument of the divine purpose; for all his heart's anguish, rewarded in full" (Isaias 53. 10–11).

The Servant is clearly an individual, but his vocation makes him one with his people; his task is concerned with a Covenant; his originality lies in developing to their maximum the characteristics of the spiritual Israel, of the *anawim*; he has been long awaited, but will also become a model for future generations; and a day will come when people will yearn to share his final destiny. The Machabean age saw a spiritual somersault. Under the blows of the persecution by Antiochus Epiphanes the best elements in Israel joined forces to defend their religion and their homes. Israel was always at its best when overwhelmed by its enemies; it always saw in such ordeals a stimulus and an invitation to surpass itself. The edict that unleashed the persecution in 167 B.C. was a providential occurrence, a *καιρός* (kairos, favourable opportunity), like the Exile and Pharaoh's persecution. The "lovers of the Law" now occupy the forefront of the stage; they are the *hasidim* or pious, whose voice can already be heard in one or two psalms. No doubt they include the *anawim*. They join the Machabees for the struggle (1 Mac. 2. 42). Among them are a number of politically-minded intellectuals, including probably the author of the book of Daniel. The stakes were high; it was a question of preserving the Covenant. The means employed were preaching and martyrdom (Dan. 11. 33–35), the very methods outlined in the prophecy of the Servant. Moreover, the names applied to these people are borrowed from the great symbolical figure: like the *Ebed*, they are "instructors" (*maskilim*: see Isaias 52. 13) and "wise counsellors" (*masdiqim*: Isaias 53. 11) who have turned to the people (*har-rabbim*: ibid.) to uplift it and win it over. Martyrdom is their lot (see also 2 Mac. 7; 14. 46; 12. 44). For them, resurrection will be the providential means of participating in the messianic era for which they will have prepared the way with their blood. With them are contrasted the apostates, doomed to eternal torment. It is true to say that the famous passage in Daniel illuminates retrospectively and democratizes the prophecy of the Servant. A selective resurrection is envisaged, in a context of national revival: "And in that hour of distress thy fellow-countrymen shall win deliverance, all whose names are found written when the record lies open. Many shall wake, that now lie sleeping in the dust of earth, some to enjoy life everlasting, some to be confronted for ever with their disgrace. Bright shall be the glory of wise counsellors, as the radiance of the sky above; starry-bright for ever their glory, who have taught many the right way" (Dan. 12. 1–3).

The passage in Isaias in which St Jerome already saw the resurrection of the martyrs (*mortui tui, qui interfecti sunt propter te*—probably the pious who were killed in the difficult times towards the end of the fourth century) should be placed in a similar context. The author is inspired by the legendary picture of Mother Earth fertilized by a heavenly dew and giving fresh life to the dead: "Fresh life they shall have, Lord, that are thine in death; lost to us, they shall live again. Awake and utter your praises, you that dwell in the dust. The dew thou sendest, Lord, shall bring light to them . . ." (Isaias 26. 19).

The resurrected dead form part of the great fresco of the Kingdom in Psalm 21: "Him shall they worship, him only, that are laid to rest in the earth, even from their dust they shall adore" (Ps. 21. 30).

These passages expressing the hope of resurrection leave many points obscure. For example, what is to be the precise state of those raised from the dead? One of the Machabean martyrs (2 Mac. 7. 11) seems to expect the restoration of his tongue and hands; but this may be too literal an interpretation of a spontaneous answer. Isaias 26. 19 and Dan. 12. 3 seem to foretell a new kind of humanity, and it seems likely that St Paul's hints (1 Cor. 15) are to be connected with these passages, which are more concerned with suggestion than description. Again, the reader wonders what the scope of the resurrection will be. Ps. 21 seems to imply that it will be universal, but the other passages suggest a selective resurrection applying only to Israel, in fact only to the just in Israel. The idea of a general resurrection was to be expressed in the fourth book of Esdras, which dates from the first century after Christ, but not as a feature of the messianic age. When the latter had arrived, a phase covering all mankind would open: general resurrection and last judgement, with heaven for the just and hell for the sinful.

It seems fairly clear, on the contrary, that in the texts we have discussed the resurrection is envisaged as applying to the Remnant of Israel, that is, as confined to the favoured domain of the Covenant and the eschatology it implies.

It seems fairly clear, too, that it was expected within the ranks of a religious group—the *hasidim-anawim*—the group which was to furnish the first martyrs.

Here we meet again a line of descent with which we have already made acquaintance. The reader will remember those pietists who placed their union with Yahweh above everything else. They lived to the full the experience of the Covenant, so that loyalty, trust and love became second nature to them. Just as the vicissitudes of history had been a test of monotheistic faith, so the trials of their individual lives brought this faith to maturity. Seen in this light, the book of Job, which dates from the fourth or fifth century B.C., acquires a lofty significance. The Job who is described in this poem stands for a whole group. He may be regarded as a mystic who, although never in danger of losing his faith (Job 6. 10), goes through a sort of dark night of the soul, at the end of which he rediscovers his God as a mystery beyond the ethical categories in which he had previously been placed. This penetration to the *Ipsissimus Deus*, the transcendent God who dwells within, finds here its loftiest expression. A reading of the book of Job will always ward off, for believers, the temptation to speak of God as though he were a subject for discussion. He is the personal God, and the believer must allow him unlimited credit in a spirit of "complete humility polarized by the very transcendence of him who is invoked"[1]: "Let him slay me if he will! I await his decree" (Job 13. 15).

This cry, which commentators tried to tone down, expresses Job's deepest feelings when confronted with death. The problem is posed in an atmosphere reminiscent of Greek tragedy. Job is just as alone as Prometheus. But the Zeus of Aeschylus is very different from the Shaddai of Job, the God upon whom one relies. It could also be said that the problem is posed on a sapiential basis: man is considered apart from his historical background; he cannot take refuge, as the

[1] G. Marcel, *Du refus à l'invocation*, p. 217.

martyrs did two centuries later, in the hope of renewed life in the messianic kingdom. His hopes do not extend beyond the span of his own life, which he expects to be prolonged as a vindication of his attitude (Job 19. 25–7). He does not affirm any belief in a happy life beyond the grave, but his religious attitude has made such an affirmation subsequently possible.

The author of Psalm 72 has been described as a "little Job". Yet the psalmist goes further than the wise man. His point of departure is the same: the ever-present scandal of the prosperity (*shalom*) of the sinful (Ps. 72. 2–12; Job 21). Surely, says the psalmist, God's justice must oblige him to grant to the just, either here on earth or elsewhere, the reward promised to virtue. But this is not the theme which the author develops. Since he belongs himself to "the company of the children of God" (v. 15), is ever at God's side (v. 23) and goes to the temple to pray (v. 17), he feels that this "communion" is unbreakable and that love aspires after eternity. The revelation which he receives in the temple assures him of this: "Thine to guide me with thy counsel, thine to welcome me into glory at last. What else does heaven hold for me, but thyself? What charm for me has earth, here at thy side? What though flesh of mine, heart of mine, should waste away? Still God will be my heart's stronghold, eternally my inheritance" (Ps. 72. 24–6).

It is impossible to point to the precise moment when this mysterious new faith first began to take shape. The idea had long been current in Israel that God had preserved certain exceptional men from death by "taking them to himself"; cases in point are those of Henoch (Gen. 5. 21) and Elias (4 Kings 2. 5–13). These "abductions" were described by the word *laqah* (to take) which is used by the psalmist here. It was already in use among the Semitic peoples to describe the apotheosis of exceptional persons like Umnapishtim, who was snatched up by Bel[2] to enjoy immortality, the prerogative of the gods. The psalmist no doubt referred to these illustrious patrons in order to express the hope that dwelt in him. We find a similar phrase in Psalm 48: "But my life (*nefech*) God will *rescue* from the power of that lower darkness (*sheol*)" (Ps. 48. 16).

These psalmists did not define in what precise way they expected their hopes to be fulfilled. They may have visualized being taken up into heaven instead of dying, as R. Kittel thinks, or else resurrection from the *sheol*. There is much to be said in favour of the second interpretation, because of the links, which we have emphasized, between these psalmists and the first groups who spoke expressly of resurrection. It is curious that the writer should not have thought already, as in Henoch 22, of the possible existence of several "mansions" in the *sheol*, with some of them reserved for the just. What is quite clear—and it is the essential point—is his certainty that God will never abandon the pious, even in death (Ps. 138. 8).

The mystical outpouring of Ps. 15 says the same thing. The author can see no end to his communion with Yahweh; his admirable phrases were to serve one day to greet the great event of Easter (Acts 2. 25–8; 13. 35). We can scarcely expect a mystical hymn to be a manual of eschatology: "Glad and merry am I, heart and soul of me; my body, too, shall rest in confidence that thou wilt not leave my soul in the place of death, or allow thy faithful servant to see corruption. Thou wilt shew me the way of life, make me full of gladness in thy presence; at thy right hand are delights that will endure for ever" (Ps. 15. 9–11).

Still another voice was to express the hope of immortality in new tones. At Alexandria in the first century before Christ

[2] Ancient god of Nippur in Sumeria, later identified with the god Marduk of Babylon. [*Trans.*]

a cultivated Jew who was somewhat tinged with Platonism spoke of the deliverance that comes with the moment of death. Perhaps the spirit here on earth is imprisoned (Plato, *Phaedo* 62b) or entombed (Plato, *Gorgias* 493a), as it were, in the body: "Ever the soul is weighed down by a mortal body, earth-bound cell that clogs the manifold activity of its thought" (Wisdom 9. 15).

No doubt this reflection no more implies a complete philosophy than the inscription on a Jewish tomb at Tell el Yehoudieh in Egypt: "This tomb conceals within it my body nurtured in purity, but the spirit has departed from it to join the saints." But at the very least this refracted anthropology borrowed from the Greek culture around him has enabled the writer to give better expression to his own message, which is the affirmation of immortality: "God, to be sure, framed man for an immortal destiny, the created image of his own endless being . . . the devil's envy brought death into the world" (Wisdom 2. 23–4).

So man is invited to become what he is; "justice", the spiritual state found where divine gift and human response meet, qualifies him to enter into the peace (Wisdom 3. 3), the rest (Wisdom 4. 7) and the salvation of living eternally in the Lord (Wisdom 5. 16). The old expressions which occur at the beginning of the biblical tradition are here used again and given a fresh meaning. Death is only a transition to a richer life, in comparison with which earthly blessings like long life (Wisdom 4. 7–18) and numerous children (Wisdom 3. 13–14) pale into insignificance. Our present life may only be a succession of tests set by God (Wisdom 3. 5–6); the important thing is that it should be lived in "wisdom", "justice" and "love", so that it becomes an introduction to immortality (*ἀφθαρσία, ἀθανασία*).

CHAPTER VIII

BIBLICAL MAN

The expression *homo biblicus* is becoming fashionable. For a portrait of this "biblical man", we only need to enumerate once again, more systematically, the characteristics which we have noted during the course of the preceding pages.

Of the marks of civilized man, he has no aptitude for philosophical thought or the expression of general ideas, no capacity for the scientific acquisition of knowledge, little artistic ability and no record of political power or success. We are apparently dealing with a Semite who is not in the forefront of his race. But he must be credited with a number of talents which were to suit him for his mission: an attention to real values, a gift for delicate observation, a taste for the land, a capacity for assimilation, the ability to tell a meaningful story, to dream, to be thrilled and to suffer, a sense of the past and of the continuity of experience, a desire to teach and communicate, a concern for the community and a taste for symbol and mystery. It should be noted that some of these characteristics are not entirely unconnected with the religious side of *homo biblicus*. There may be religious grounds for the lack of interest in art (Exod. 20. 4); and, conversely, a certain cultural poverty, a certain ignorance of secondary causes can open the heart to God. It is quite clear that the Israelite's spiritual qualities fitted him for a religious vocation and, conversely, were to be refined by it.

The reader must also have noticed in the course of these

pages what might be described as the antinomies of biblical man: a taste for tradition combined with yearning for the new, a sense of the Book which crystallizes and yet also of the living Word, collectivism and individualism, separatism and a sense of mission. To understand these contradictions we must see how biblical man lives; for the key to them lies in the unity of an intense religious life.

Biblical man is the man whose heart is open to God. That is the secret of his daily life. What we should look for in the Bible, which is the map of a spiritual journey, are the original religious attitudes, the lasting orientations which have a symbolic value and can therefore be universalized. The way in which such truths are expressed is eventually canonized and accepted as a norm. Our task is to turn to account, when a civilization is outstripped, what still remains basic and eternal. As Pius XI said, "Spiritually we are all Semites".

Biblical man is man before God. Elias' cry, "as the Lord I serve is a living God" (3 Kings 18. 15), is the outburst of faith in a moment of crisis. Faith carries a man beyond the distress that turns him pale; it gives him a fixed and firm support to lean on in security. Israel lived in this attitude, intensely, without reasoning about it. It was the basic fact with which St Paul linked the two Testaments (Rom. 4), like his disciple, the author of the epistle to the Hebrews (Heb. 11). St John echoes it in his famous phrase: "Our faith, that is the triumphant principle which triumphs over the world" (1 John 5. 4).

The Bible is the book which gives us a sense of God.

Because biblical man stands before God, he does not feel himself a prey to the dark, demonic forces reckoned to be at work in the universe (Ps. 90. 5–6). He looks upon history as the scene of a dialogue with God. When his glance comes to rest on the vanity of human endeavour and causes him to question the meaning of life, his faith enables him to look beyond the absurdity of the world. Even Ecclesiastes, who is in many ways exceptional, retains this fundamental faith in a God who keeps his secrets to himself. To take a few concrete examples, biblical man is, first and foremost, Abraham in the unexpected situation noted in Heb. 11. 8–9—leaving a settled life to become a nomad, having a son in his old age and then sacrificing this promised son; the Isaias of 701 B.C., staking all on God in the throes of a siege lost in advance (Isaias 38); Habacuc, in the middle of a Babylonian invasion, triumphing in the deliverance God sends him (Hab. 3. 18); above all, Job, at grips with his undeserved suffering and the theologians of his time, a panting Job who, deprived of God's retributions, at any rate never loses sight of God himself; and, last of all, the psalmist whose faith conquers even the tragedy of death (Ps. 73. 13).

These various refusals to despair, this recovery of a feeling of security in the world by appeals to a power above it, are only a few examples of an habitual attitude which reflects the deep instincts of biblical man. We have watched him at prayer; its perfection consists in an inward attitude of attention and silence before the Lord. We have watched his struggle in the field of morality, a struggle that lies at the heart of a drama in which God speaks and man hears or rejects an appeal from on high.

Biblical man never stands alone before God, but always amid brothers, for he is the man of the Covenant. This basic fact has, I think, been fairly strongly emphasized in the foregoing pages. The constant aim was to build up a community possessing the sense of a spiritual task, to explore more and more thoroughly the people's vocation as witness and missionary, to sharpen the sense of personal responsibility when, within the bosom of Israel, one felt "called" (the prophets and their disciples, Isaias 8. 16, 18; the priests of Zach. 3. 8; the *anawim* of Ps. 149. 4; the *hasidim* of 1 Mac. 2. 42; the "wise counsellors" and the martyrs of Dan. 11. 33, 35).

This communal aspect of salvation had a special importance in the lives of some men. The theme of vocation is an eminently biblical one. Vocation makes the prophets responsible for their brothers just as Moses, their prototype, was (Num. 11. 12). We find, then, a succession of men with a special kind of responsibility, especially when we arrive at the crucial period when Israel had lost its previous institutions, the king being a prisoner and the priest without employment. In the spiritual community of the exile the prophets provide the new organization of God's people; they are the mediators, as it were, and rallying-points. They do not always feel fitted for this responsibility, whose real weight they gradually discover. Loving one's brother, in the case of Jeremias or Ezechiel, means doing all one can to put them in contact with the divine message, bearing the worry of their sins and interceding for them. It means feeling that God will call each of them to account. It means facing despair and discouragement, for suffering is the price of spiritual responsibility of this kind. Amid setbacks and failures, the bearer of such a responsibility feels how near his vocation brings him to others and also how alone among them it leaves him. Intimacy with Yahweh divides him from sinners but also sends him back to them.

Israel's greatness lies in having accepted the office of God's collaborator, and in having discharged it with better and better qualifications. The temptation here was that of yielding to pride. The first form of this temptation—and it was endemic—was to convert the talents bestowed by God into property, to regard the Covenant as a mainly human enterprise, to have the impression of "rallying in the Lord's cause" (Judges 5. 23); in short, to forget the senior partner in favour of the human partner, who was resolved to win a place in the sun. It is possible to recite the *Yahve beqirbenu!* ("The Lord of hosts is with us") (Amos 5. 14; Ps. 45. 4, 6, 8, 12) as a sort of "*Gott mit uns*", and to make it merely the accompaniment to a national will-to-survival. The temptation was all the stronger since the Kingdom of God—the purpose of the Covenant—first came into being in the form of a very earthly kingdom, suitably equipped with mercenary armies and political alliances. Until the coming of Christ, the Church coincided with the people of Israel, whose necessary but dangerous aims linked religious values to temporal blessings, and emphasized only too often the latter, which man can claim to achieve by his own strength. The prophets fought the good fight against this "humanization" of God's plan. They repeated tirelessly that Israel was nothing and God everything, that the success of the chosen people was primarily his work, that it depended not on arms or force, but on his spirit (Zach. 4. 6), that the Lord's hand could reach far as ever to bring deliverance (Isaias 59. 1), that the creation and the successive liberations of Israel were redemptions, and that the Covenant was a grace. Humility, gratitude and recourse to God are Israel's duties. But this grace, once received, stimulates to activity; the same background produced both the book of Daniel, with its invitation to wait, and the *Hasidim*, who joined the Machabees to set up the Kingdom by force. For the Kingdom is both "gift" and "task".

We have seen that the same temptation to pride can assail biblical man in the sphere of private morality, and that, here too, Jeremias, Ezechiel and the *anawim* taught him the humility that inspires a spiritual life truly centred on God. As St Paul puts it, "no human creature was to have any ground for boasting, in the presence of God" (1 Cor. 1. 29).

Modern man may feel a little bewildered when confronted with this description, which we have purposely confined to essentials. He will also notice a certain harmony with some of his own reactions and points of view. The Marxist has rediscovered the thrill of participation in an adventure greater than himself which may be described as a counterpart of the biblical messianic hope. In his eyes, however, history is not a dialogue with Transcendence; it obeys its own immanent laws. The wheel of history crushes man, whose dignity counts for nothing. The existentialist has rediscovered the condition of man, with all its frustrations and the final tragedy of death, and has tried to extol freedom. He agrees with biblical man in his recognition of the frustrations inherent in human life, but the latter has surmounted the tragedy and taken confidence before death itself. Scientific humanism in its turn runs the risk of giving man the feeling that he is becoming master of his own destiny and of robbing him of the need for God. *Homo laicus*, so common today, is the man who, rejecting the idea of transcendence, has lost not only the secret of making appeals to a higher power but even the desire to make them. This kind of man has to be taught or retaught the elementary attitudes of biblical man. If "man is a demand for meaning", he must be made to understand that God is the meaning of the world and the meaning of man, and initiated into the humility and "poverty" that express our ontological condition. The great strength of biblical man is his faith, whence springs his activity in the world, his equilibrium and the optimism known as hope.

Biblical man was the product of a long and gradual process of instruction. It has not been possible to describe this process in full, but only to allude to it. To tell the whole story, it would have been necessary to call up a long line of biblical characters in accordance with Jewish procedure (see, for example, Ben Sirach's sacred history in Ecclus. 44–50, or the catalogue of the "men who went before" in Heb. 11).

The Bible rarely gives us details of their lives; its interest in them is not the biographical interest of a Plutarch. It only makes exceptions for a few men like David, Jeremias and

Nehemias. More often the people it puts before us are the incarnation of some essential characteristic, which is recalled and emphasized many times in order to engrave it on the reader's heart. They are the sort of characters who appear in stained-glass windows: Abraham, the man of faith; Moses, the man with a great responsibility; Esdras, the stickler for duty; Job, the man with entire faith in God; Daniel, the man of hope. Echoes of their times, pioneers of the future, they dot the whole course of the Old Testament. There is an underlying link between them: they are all men of the Covenant.

Some of them live on intensely in tradition. Moses gives life to the whole Bible; David becomes the patron of the *anawim*; Solomon that of the wise men; and Esdras that of the scribes.

Schools and groups sprang into being under their influence. There was a school of Isaias which flourished from the prophet's time onwards and adopted his attitude of humility before the "Holy One of Israel"; a Deuteronomic school which went back beyond the Levites of the eighth century right to Moses for its interpretation of history and its conception of the people of God; and a priestly school which prided itself on its attachment to Aaron. There were probably regroupings after the exile; wise men, *hasidim* and *anawim* all cherished similar ideals. Today we can also see the similarities between two groups who were formerly—and rather short-sightedly—regarded as distinct: prophets and priests of ancient times.

The Old Testament invites us to admire this unity in diversity. In very different situations the men of the Bible all reacted in accordance with the Covenant. Whether they are outstanding or anonymous figures, they become symbolical. At the end of the line St Matthew's gospel (1. 16) places Mary, the link between the two Covenants, humanity's purest flower, appearing before God with nothing but her poverty, her prayer, her joy and her welcome for the coming of God.

Jesus is the biblical man *par excellence*, and at the end of this study the believing Christian will turn his glance towards him.

No one has prayed as Jesus did (Luke 11. 1). But he addresses the Father in the actual phrases of the Psalms: the psalms of pilgrimage, the paschal Hallels (hymns of praise), and, above all, those prayers of poverty and trust which he utters on the cross, at the moment of death: "Father, into thy hands I commend my spirit" (Ps. 30. 6; Luke 23. 46). At this point Ps. 21 enables him to express both his distress and his hope (Mark 15. 34). St Augustine was certainly justified in describing Jesus as *Iste Cantator Psalmorum*. Similarly, Jesus used again, with varying depths of meaning, the parables of the wise men, the obscure language of the apocalyptic writers (Mark 13), the vigorous harangues of the prophets (Matt. 23) and even their striking modes of behaviour (Mark 11. 13 ff.). He was completely at home in the Bible.

He also read his mission in it. The sublimest pages of the Old Testament rose spontaneously to his memory at the great turning-points in his life. On the day when he stood up to read in the synagogue at Nazareth (Luke 4. 16), he borrowed the programme of preaching to the poor from Isaias 61; at the time of the Galilean set-back, Isaias 53 was at the back of his mind (Mark 8. 31), as it was at the Last Supper (Mark 14. 21); and at the moment of sacrifice Ps. 21 expressed what he felt. It was not just chance that he who was bound by no prophecy should have wished to fulfil those which placed him in the priestly stream of human suffering. But this suffering led to Easter and victory.

Jesus knows how to read the Scriptures because he fulfils them. He is their real centre, their final secret, the key to their meaning. In him, biblical man reaches his full stature.

SELECT BIBLIOGRAPHY

An asterisk denotes works by non-Catholic writers

1. *The Old Testament in general*

STEINMUELLER, J. E., and SULLIVAN, K.: *A Companion to the Old Testament*, London, Herder, and New York, Wagner, 1946.

*ROWLEY, H. H. (Ed.): *The Old Testament and Modern Study*, Oxford and New York, Oxford Univ. Press, 1951.

2. *History of Israel*

DANIEL-ROPS: *Israel and the Ancient World* (translated from the French), London, Eyre and Spottiswoode, and New York, Longmans, 1949.

*PEDERSEN, J.: *Israel: its Life and Culture*, Oxford and New York, Oxford Univ. Press, 1953.

GROLLENBERG, L. H.: *Atlas of the Bible*, translated and edited by H. H. Rowley and J. M. H. Reid, London and New York, Nelson, 1956.

3 *The Covenant*

*ROWLEY, H. H.: *The Biblical Doctrine of Election*, London, Lutterworth Press, 1950, and Naperville, Illinois, Allenson, 1952.

4. *Old Testament Theology and Morality*

HEINISCH, P.: *Theology of the Old Testament* (translated from the German by W. Heidt), Collegeville, Minn., the Liturgical Press, 1950.

*PORTEOUS, N. W.: *The Basis of the ethical Teaching of the Prophets* in *Studies in Old Testament Prophecy* (ed. H. H. Rowley), Edinburgh, T. and T. Clark, 1950.

*TAYLOR, C.: *Sayings of the Jewish Fathers*, Cambridge, University Press, 1897.

5. *Prayer and Public Worship*

BIRD, T. E.: *Commentary on the Psalms*, London, Burns Oates, 1927.

*WELCH, A. C.: *Prophet and Priest in Old Israel*, Oxford and New York, Oxford Univ. Press, 1953.

6. *The Messianic Hope*

*MOWINCKEL, S.: *He that Cometh*, Oxford and New York, Oxford University Press, 1956.

7. *The Missionary Ideal*

*ROWLEY, H. H.: *The Missionary Message of the Old Testament*, 2nd edition, London, Carey Kingsgate Press, 1955.

8. *Life after Death*

SUTCLIFFE, E. F., S.J.: *The Old Testament and the Future Life*, London, Burns Oates, and Westminster, Maryland, Newman Press, 1946.

*JOHNSON, A. R.: *The Vitality of the Individual in the Thought of Ancient Israel*, Cardiff, University of Wales Press, 1949.

9. *Biblical Man*

CHARLIER, C.: *The Christian Approach to the Bible*, translated from the French by H. J. Richards, L.S.S., and B. Peters, S.T.L., London, Sands, 1958.